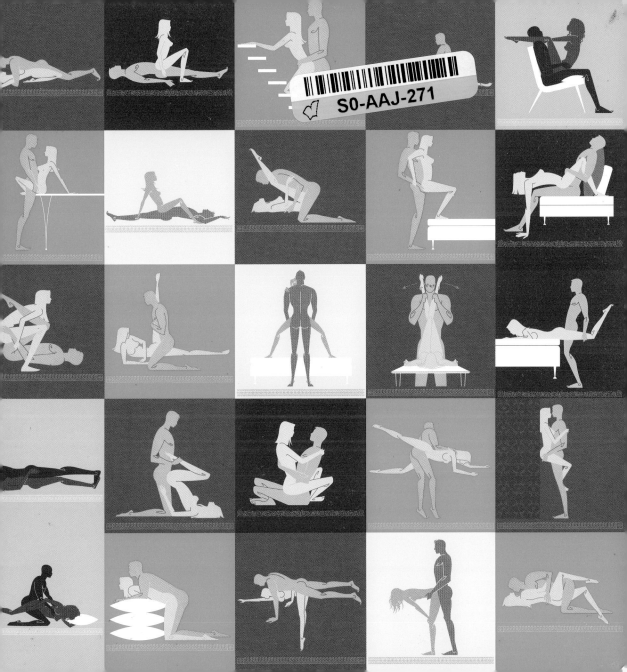

S0-AAJ-271

# THE COSMO KAMA SUTRA

## 77 mind-blowing sex positions

## The Editors of COSMOPOLITAN

HEARST BOOKS

A division of Sterling Publishing Co., Inc.

New York / London
**www.sterlingpublishing.com**

Cosmopolitan The Cosmo Kama Sutra
77 Mind-Blowing Sex Positions

The Library of Congress cataloged the hardcover edition as follows:
Cosmopolitan : the Cosmo Kama Sutra : 77 mind-blowing sex positions
p. cm.
ISBN 978-1-58816-423-0
1. Sex instruction. 2. Sex customs. 3. Sexual intercourse. I. Cosmopolitan (New York, N.Y. : 1952)
HQ31.C827 2005
631.9'6—dc22      2004052640

10  9  8  7  6  5  4  3  2  1

Illustrations by Bo Lundberg
Cover Design by Chris Thompson
Book Design by Celia Fuller, Peter Perron and Theresa Izzillo
Edited by Isabel Burton and John Searles
Additional text by Sara Bodnar, Cara Litke and Elizabeth Holmes

First paperback edition published 2009

Published by Hearst Books,
A division of Sterling Publishing Co., Inc.
387 Park Avenue South, New York, NY 10016

www.cosmopolitan.com

For information about custom editions, special sales, premium and corporate purchases,
please contact Sterling Special Sales Department at 800-805-5489 or specialsales@sterlingpublishing.com.

Distributed in Canada by Sterling Publishing
c/o Canadian Manda Group, 165 Dufferin Street
Toronto, Ontario, Canada M6K 3H6

Distributed in Australia by Capricorn Link (Australia) Pty. Ltd.
P.O. Box 704, Windsor, NSW 2756 Australia

Manufactured in China

Sterling ISBN 978-1-58816-747-7

# Contents

## ■ Lust Lessons

# Preface

Welcome to *Cosmo's* version of the Kama Sutra. It's a tantalizing, eye-opening, and inspiring guide to 77 of the most exciting sex positions imaginable.

Chances are you've heard of the Kama Sutra, the ancient Indian sex handbook. Over the years in *Cosmopolitan*, we've presented some of its classic carnal configurations with our own special spin. Readers repeatedly tell us that our features on the Kama Sutra are among their favorites in the magazine. We thought it would be helpful to compile all these positions (and *more!*) in one book so that you always have them at your fingertips.

If you're like most people, you have certain positions in your sexual repertoire that you return to again and again because you thoroughly enjoy them and they're the most likely to guarantee you maximum pleasure. But repeatedly falling back on the same positions can leave you in a romp rut. A truly satisfying sex life calls for periodic experimentation, for being adventurous within the parameters of what's comfortable for you as an individual and as a couple.

Peruse these pages and you'll discover adventurous positions like the Figure Eight (page 15) and the G-Spot Jiggy (page 41), which were designed for maximum female pleasure in mind. A position like Romp With a View (page 89) is fabulous for your guy because it offers him plenty of eye-candy. By using muscles you didn't even know you had, the Rock-a-Bye Booty (page 17) will drive him wild in ways that might surprise you both! As you embark on your erotic journey through these positions, you'll discover that the sometimes subtle differences between them can introduce brand new sensations. To help guide you, each Kama Sutra position comes with a carnal challenge rating—the more flames the more advanced the pose and the hotter the payoff. And there's a bonus! Our Lust Lessons will give you the lowdown on everything from pre-sex stretches that help you limber up to secret hot spots on his body and yours.

So if you're up for the challenge (and I never met a *Cosmo* reader who wasn't), this guide can help transform your lust life from Oh my! to OMIGOD! Our epic exotic collection awaits you.

*Kate White*

Editor-in-Chief, *Cosmopolitan*

# Straddle His Saddle

## ◼ Erotic Instructions:

Have your guy sit on the floor with his arms stretched out behind him for support and his legs crossed loosely Indian-style. Climb onto his lap so you're straddling him in a kneeling position and hold on to his shoulders as you lower yourself onto his erect penis. Lean toward him and keep your bodies close together as you take control of the timing and speed of the thrusting...Ride him, cowgirl!

## ◼ Why You'll Love It:

This is the ultimate girl-power position in *The Cosmo Kama Sutra*, because you command the action by alternating slow, shallow strokes with deep thrusts. To mix thing up more, lower yourself down your man's shaft in drive-him-nuts circular motions (like a corkscrew), and this seriously simple sack-session becomes one wild ride. You'll be facing him, so the hot and heavy eye contact will make the action extra steamy.

**COSMO HINT**

With you in charge of the speed and depth, you can tease the supersensitive head of his penis and tantalize the lower third of your vagina, which is packed with excitable nerve endings. Then, just when he's about to explode in ecstasy, take his entire penis inside you for a sensational suprise.

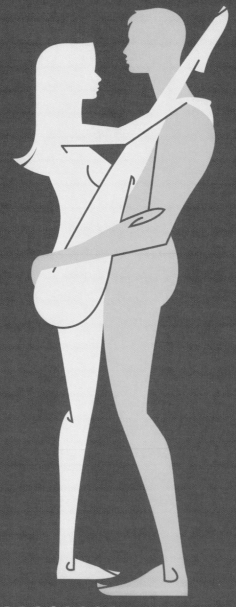

# The Lusty Leg Lift

## ■ Erotic Instructions:

Face your partner, standing with your legs shoulder width apart. Take your left foot and turn it out to the side while keeping your right one facing forward. Have him widen his stance, with his legs about three feet apart, and then ask him to bend his knees ever-so-slightly. Wrap your arms around his neck and have him put his arms snugly around your lower back. Here's where it gets a little tricky: Pull your right leg up and place your right foot on his left shoulder, keeping your right knee bent. As he slowly enters you, ease into the vertical split by sliding your calf as far up his left shoulder as you comfortably can.

## ■ Why You'll Love It:

There's a reason guys are drawn to a kick line of cheerleaders: Flexibility is h-o-t. Most men are so stiff, they think a knee bend is an Olympic feat—so pull this one on him and he'll worship you as a sex goddess who knows how to stretch sexual boundaries.

**COSMO HINT** Pressing your man up against a wall will help both of you keep your balance and force him to relinquish all power over to you. To him, there's no bigger turn-on than a hot chick who's not afraid to take charge and tell him what to do.

# Figure-Eight

## ▉ Erotic Instructions:

Lie on the floor faceup with a couple of pillows propping your butt. Keep your knees half bent, your legs splayed wide, and your arms high over your head or holding on to his side (as in the picture)—so that your body is extremely open. Have your partner enter you at a higher angle than usual (the pillows will help), planting his hands on the floor beside your head. He should move inside you with slow, languid figure-eight motions, so that you feel his whole package—his penis plus pubic region. Remember: The figure eight motion is key to this maneuver.

## ▉ Why You'll Love It:

You get double the orgasmic pleasure: His penis's circular motions tantalize your vagina while his pubic bone lightly rubs against your clitoris. This is a slow-building, easy-orgasm position that allows you to lie back and let him please you with long, sensual strokes, until you climb to a powerful peak.

**COSMO HINT** For a surefire G-spot trigger, pile up the pillows. The more you have propping you up, the easier it is for him to penetrate you deeply. And not only will your orgasms be even more intense, but you'll also satisfy every inch of his member—so there's even the potential for a simultaneous climax!

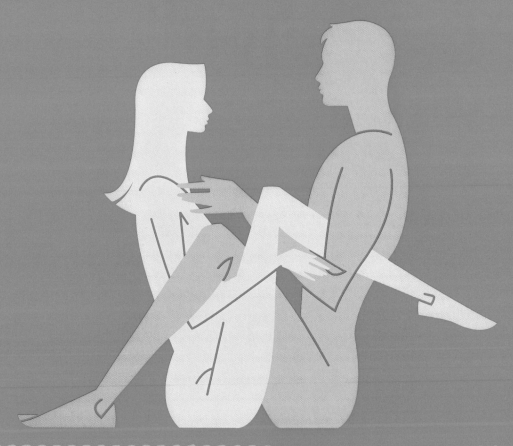

# Rock-a-Bye Booty

## ■ Erotic Instructions:

With your man on his back, slowly straddle him. Once he's inside you, have him lift up his torso and position yourselves so that you're sitting face-to-face. Wrap your legs tightly around his buttocks and have him do the same to you. Then both you and your guy should link your elbows under the other person's knees and lift them up to chest level. Cradle each other in bear-hug fashion.

## ■ Why You'll Love It:

Even though this position limits the thrusting possibilities, you can rock each other's world by swaying back and forth. Start out slow, get the rhythm down, and then let loose. As you build momentum, keep him hard by squeezing your PC muscles—the same ones that contract when you cut off the flow of urine. This will tighten your hold on his member while increasing blood flow to your nether regions, boosting both your bliss.

**COSMO HINT** Because you and your guy are so close, this position is perfect for more intimate moments. The added face time opens up a slew of steamy smooching possibilities—so get even closer by kissing his neck or sucking on his earlobe as you move in sync.

# On-the-Edge

## ■ Erotic Instructions:

Sit your man on the edge of the bed, with his legs dangling freely. With your hands on his shoulders, lean him onto a stack of pillows to support his lower back. Kneel astride his hips and lower yourself onto his erect member. Brace your hands on the pillows behind your partner's head for added leverage and support.

## ■ Why You'll Love It:

The On-the-Edge is sure to send you *over* the edge because you control both the depth of penetration and the intensity of clitoral stimulation. He'll love it because it gives him a chance to reach around and let his hands wander—have him use the pads of his fingers to tickle your butt, back, and thighs. Plus, he's in prime position to caress your buttocks and to stroke and kiss your breasts, face, and neck.

**COSMO HINT** Your lips are conveniently placed next to his ear, so whisper a flirty fantasy you've had about him. Add all the details you can think of—where you two are, what you're each wearing, and, of course, how much you want him. Keep your voice sexy and breathy while tickling his earlobe with your tongue.

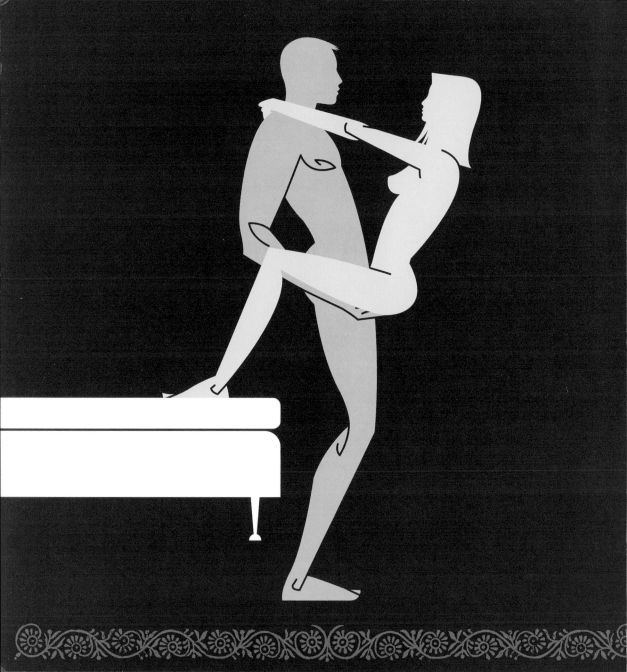

# Pleasure Pick-Me-Up

## ■ Erotic Instructions:

Standing with his back against the edge of the bed (or even the washer or dryer), your guy picks you up with his hands cradling your bottom and the backs of your thighs. Wrap your legs around his waist (place your feet on the bed for support) and your arms around his neck and shoulders. As his penis enters you, you hang suspended from him, bouncing up and down with the help of his arms.

## ■ Why You'll Love It:

For those who love a real hunk, get ready for a tawdry treat, since you'll be bound in his strong arms, swinging and swaying and absolutely at his orgasmic mercy. And the rapid-fire bouncy action provides a brand-new move—less in-and-out, and more up-and-down. As he thrusts against your front vaginal wall, you're near enough for longing looks and deep kisses.

**COSMO HINT**

Squeeze your thighs around his waist, lock your hands behind his neck, then carefully arch your back so your pelvic region nestles fimrly with his. This wanton whimsical pose will up the erotic ante for you both.

# Now and Zen

## ■ Erotic Instructions:

This pose provides a quiet moment in the middle of the mattress madness. When on the brink of the Big O, take a break from whatever heart-pounding position you're in and try this out as a horny holding pattern. Roll onto your sides, face-to-face (if possible, keep him inside you the entire time), then put the passion on a low simmer with your legs intertwined and your chests pressed against one another. Slowly build yourself back up to an even more incredible climax. Trust us, you'll both be screaming ohmmm…my…God!

## ■ Why You'll Love It:

There's not a whole lot of motion, which is why Now and Zen delays your orgasm. But it's perfect for erotic embraces and intimate contact. You'll feel closer to your man because you two are facing body-to-body. It's this kind of incredible emotional ecstasy that makes you laugh, cry, and come all at the same time.

**COSMO HINT** To up the intensity and to keep him from going (yikes!) soft on you, get into a gentle pelvic rhythm and look into each other's eyes while taking natural, deep breaths. To drive him really wild, move your body up his penis until it's just about to slip out, pause, and then take him all the way inside you.

# The Octopus

## ■ Erotic Instructions:

Have your guy sit on the floor with his hands on the ground behind him. Tell him to spread his legs and bend them slightly at the knees. Keeping your hands on the floor for support, straddle his lap, facing him, and raise your legs so your right leg rests on his left shoulder and your left leg on his right shoulder. Do it right and you two will look like a multi-limbed lust creature.

## ■ Why You'll Love It:

Because your body is tilted upward, your guy enters you in up-and-down motions rather than circular or side-to-side, bringing on deep direct G-spot orgasms. And you both get a prime bird's-eye view of the action—a male fantasy come true! Plus, if you can master this one, you two will have entered the Kama Sutra Hall of Fame. And what could be hotter than that?

**COSMO HINT** This position is all about intimate contact, so make the most of it! If you're feeling extra flexible, try wrapping your arms around his neck to get even closer to his hot body, where you can focus your attention on kissing and nibbling his lips, neck, and earlobes.

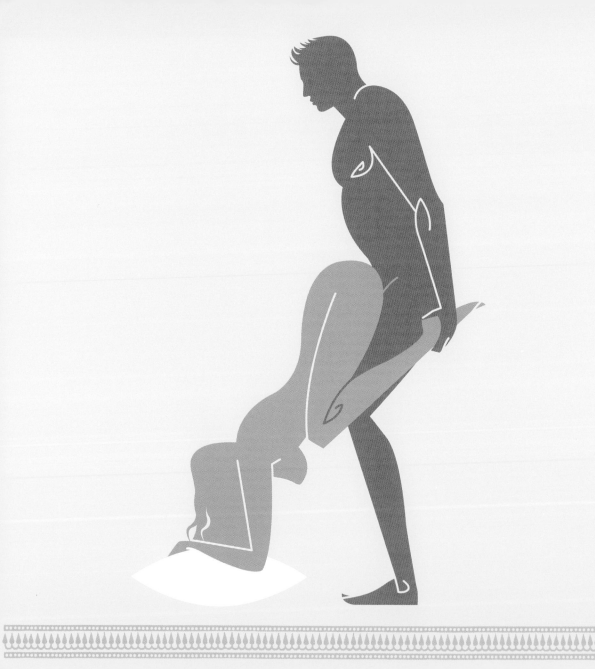

# Head Over Heels

## ▌ Erotic Instructions:

Start by lowering yourself to your knees and crossing your arms on the ground in front of you, using a pillow to cushion your elbows. Stick your butt in the air and rest your head on your arms, bracing it on the floor if you need to. Tell your man to stand behind you and lift your legs up by your ankles until your body is almost perpendicular to the floor. Keep your knees bent and have him enter you from behind.

## ▌ Why You'll Love It:

Two words: deep impact. This position has all the benefits of any rear-entry move, with the bonus of gravity on your side. Encourage him to take the plunge by telling him exactly how good his member feels. Plus, your practically upside-down body position will give the whole experience a brand new spin.

**COSMO HINT** Have him swivel his hips while he's inside you. The combination of the new angle and the added movement will excite some hot spots you never knew you had. His penis will be stimulated from every angle, too, ensuring a mind-blowing climax for the both of you, and maybe even at the same time.

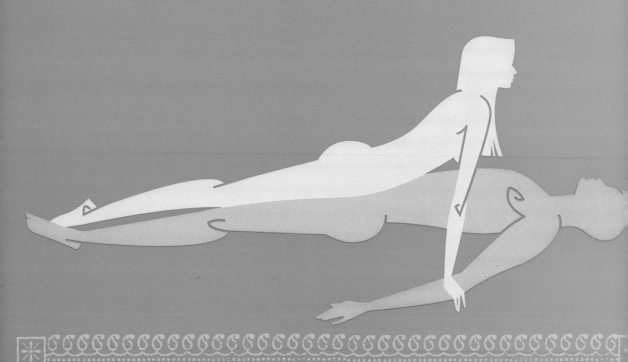

# The Python

## ■ Erotic Instructions:

Have your lover lie flat on his back with his legs together and his arms at his sides. Straddle him on your knees and lower yourself onto his penis. Once he's fully inside you, slowly stretch out so you're lying straight on top of him, aligned limb-to-limb. Grasp his hands in yours and together move your arms out to your sides. Before you start to slither around, lift your torso like a snake ready to strike. For added leverage, ask him to keep his feet flexed, then push against them with your toes.

## ■ Why You'll Love It:

You and your man are connecting on just about every inch of your bodies. With your nipples tickling his chest, your hands tightly in his grasp, and your thighs starting a fire against his, you two are sexually skin-chronized. The booty bonus: The whole time, your clitoris will be stimulated in addition to the penetration.

**COSMO HINT** Work a little magic with your tongue, bobbing your head down every so often to lick the inside of his lips. If you're feeling extra slinky, before getting in position, trace an imaginary line from his toes all the way to his kisser—making certain pit stops along the way.

# Pre-Sex Stretches

Limber up before you try any body-bending poses.

### The Spine Tingler

**Upper, middle, and lower back**

Kneel on the floor with your butt positioned on the soles of your feet. Lean forward, resting your torso on top of your thighs and stretching your arms out in front of you to loosen the muscles along your spine. Have your partner stand directly behind you and gently press on your back to enhance the stretch. For an added bonus, ask your guy for a mini shoulder massage, too. Then, switch places and return the favor.

### The Pinball Tilt

**Front of hips, abs, and thighs**

Lie on your back with your knees bent, and your feet flat on the floor. Rest your arms along your sides, and have your partner kneel beside you. As you slowly raise your pelvis off the floor, have him place his hands under you to help you hold the posture. It's important to make absolutely certain that your hips and thighs are in line so you're not over-arching. Hold for two seconds, then slowly lower yourself back down to the floor and repeat.

### The See-Saw

**Inner thigh, lower back, arms, abs**

Sit on the bed or the floor facing each other, keeping your backs straight and tall. With his legs straight and spread in a wide V, extend your legs and place your feet along his inner thighs. Then clasp hands, and look directly into each other's eyes. Maintaining eye contact, lean back as far as you can while he leans in toward you and vice versa. Take turns leaning forward and back. Switch inside and outside legs and then repeat.

# LUBE LOWDOWN

Cosmo compiled this five-point primer
to help you pick out the perfect motion lotion.

**1**

**Use water-based.** Avoid oil-based moisturizers like massage oil or petroleum jelly. These grease-mongers stain sheets, and they can cause condoms to break, putting you in line for an STD or pregnancy. Petroleum bacteria could cause an infection.

**2**

**Stick with silicone.** When you're ready to rock and roll, you want a lube that's thin, sticky, and slippery—so shop for one containing silicone, which mimics your natural wetness.

**3**

**Take a waiver on the flavor.** Products come in all kinds of tempting flavors, colors, and scents. But the more ingredients in a lubricant, the greater your chances of having an allergic reaction or developing an infection.

**4**

**Skip the spermicide.** Some lubes contain the sperm assassin nonoxynol-9, which can irritate the vagina, making sex uncomfortable. If you've had a bad experience with spermicide in the past, look for lubes that leave it out.

**5**

**Heighten his sensation.** If your man gripes about the fake feel of his condom, pull this sexy trick: Before he puts it on, apply a drop of lube inside the tip. The extra wetness will make it feel closer to the real thing.

*Source: Barbara Bartolic, M.D.

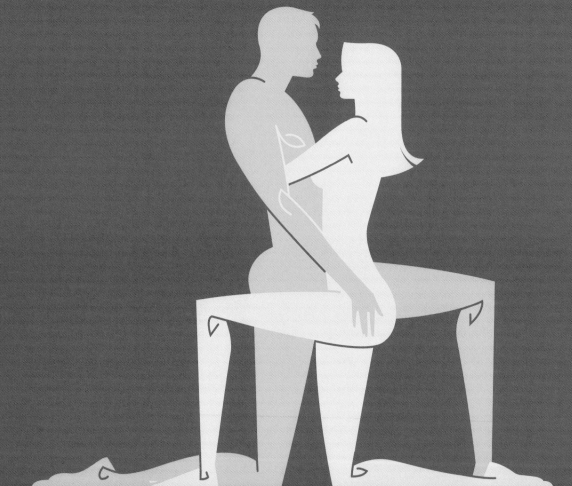

# The Passion Pretzel

## ■ Erotic Instructions:

To get into this twisted position, bring him to his knees, right from the start. Both you and your lover should start by kneeling face-to-face. Each of you should place the opposite foot flat on the ground and nudge closer, joining genitals. Leaning forward on your planted feet, both of you lunge back and forth for a slow, upright romp.

## ■ Why You'll Love It:

This pretzel pose is the ultimate in carnal equality: You're both in the exact same stance and share the reins when it comes to blowing each other's minds. While there won't be a lot of in-and-out action, your slow torso-to-torso grind provides great clitoral contact and allows a more gradual ascent to climactic cloud nine. And since both his and your arms feel free to roam, just think of the places—backsides, testicles, breasts—they can go.

**COSMO HINT**

When you both just can't take it any longer, abandon the Pretzel. While you keep the movement building, throw your knee on the ground over his bent leg and pump harder. With your arms around his neck and your legs around his buttocks, you two will be as close as can be as you climax together.

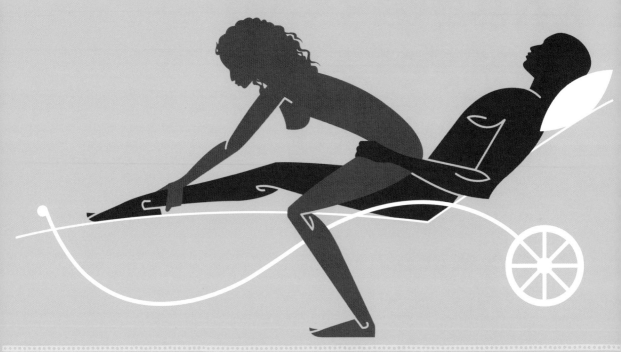

# Randy Recliner

## ▣ Erotic Instructions:

This move requires a little equipment prep. Find a reclining lawn chair or bench (narrow enough for you to get your legs around), or line up three backless chairs. Have your man lie down with his arms at his side and his legs together. Facing his toes, straddle his lap and plant both feet on the ground. Next, back yourself down onto his penis. Start moving your hips, back and forth, up and down, and side-to-side—all while he enjoys the killer view of your pivoting posterior.

## ▣ Why You'll Love It:

This fresh entry angle gives you a sweet new sensation on the back wall of your vagina. Move your booty in circular motions around his penis to hit all your pleasure spots. Make sure not to hold back in the sound department so you both know how much the other is enjoying this randy recline ride.

**COSMO HINT** Here's a way to send you both soaring: Fondle his testicles, his perineum (the area between his anus and his testicles), and your clitoris in one long, slow feel with your free hand. The extra attention to these most sensitive spots will enable the two of you to build up to outta-this-world orgasms.

# Get Down On It

## ■ Erotic Instructions:

Help your partner get comfortable in the traditional lotus position, with his legs crossed and each of his heels atop the opposite knee. Facing him, sit in his lap and mount him, with your legs wrapped snugly around his waist. Embrace each other and lock lips with a shared breath, so that as you exhale your guy inhales and vice versa. As you breathe in, rock your pelvis back and tighten your vaginal muscles. As you exhale, rock your pelvis forward and release. Your guy should mirror your movements.

## ■ Why You'll Love It:

Yoga fanatics, this one couldn't be more perfect for you. Syncing up your breathing and moving together while in this position will deepen your intimacy as you both ride the wave to a mind-blowing climax.

**COSMO HINT** Take your time getting into this couldn't-be-closer position. Relaxation is key. First, set the perfect mood with scented candles and soothing music. Then loosen each other up with sexy full-body massages. Enhance your rub with some aromatic oils, ensuring that both of you are slicked down.

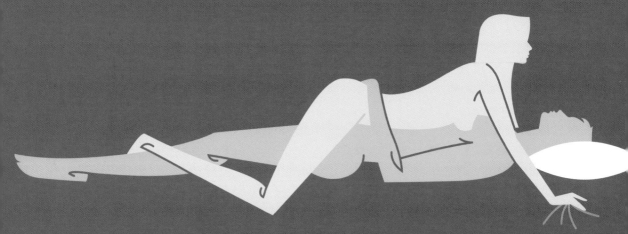

# The Ride of Your Life

## ■ Erotic Instructions:

Your guy lies on his back. Facing him, lower yourself onto his penis in a kneeling position. Keeping your knees on the bed, curl your feet around the inside of his legs, likely around his knees. Lean forward and grab the bedsheets on either side of his head. While holding the sheets—and your feet wrapped around your man's calves—squeeze your butt, tilt your pelvis, and move in small, tight motions.

## ■ Why You'll Love It:

Giddy up! By gripping the bedsheets and using the self-created "stirrups," this quasi-cowgirl configuration offers lots of leverage—you'll maintain a steady rhythm without losing momentum before reaching orgasmville. And since your body is positioned higher than in the typical girl-on-top, your clitoris can easily rub against his pubic bone.

**COSMO HINT**

By grinding in quick, controlled motions, your private parts stay in constant contact with his, making you and your man feel oh-so carnally connected. You can up the ante as you like, taking the wild ride from slow and sweet to bucking bronco. Best of all, you get to pick the pace.

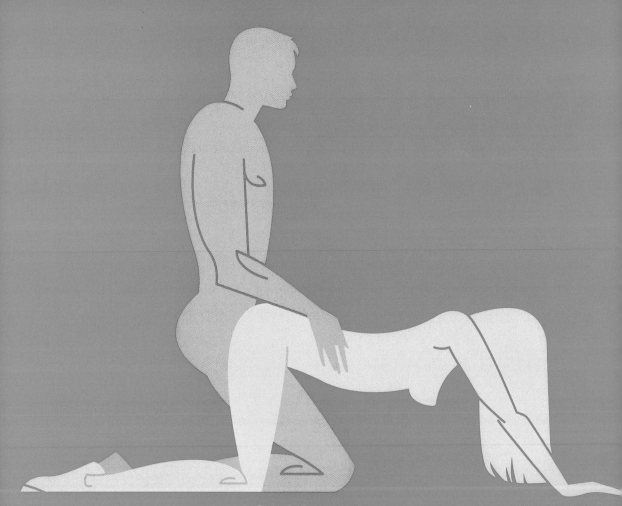

# G-Spot Jiggy

## ■ Erotic Instructions:

Not just any position will do the G-spot job: For his penis to hit your hidden hot button, your vagina has to be precisely angled. And this doggy-style penetration fits the bill perfectly. Get down on all fours with your man kneeling behind you and have him plunge inside you, grabbing your rear for balance. A little firm, well-placed stroking of this pleasure place can open up a whole new orgasmic world. If he's the exploring kind, encourage him to thrust far enough inside you so that his testicles hit your buttocks. There's something very primal about doing the deed from behind that brings out the animal in even the most mild-mannered guy.

## ■ Why You'll Love It:

Once you have a G-spot orgasm, you'll crave more. Although you may already be able to find your hot button during solo sessions (if not, see page 55), reaching it through intercourse will introduce you to a whole new level of lust.

**COSMO HINT** If the doggy-style pose doesn't make you hot enough, accessorize! Using a vibrator will definitely amp up the action. Plus, bringing a toy between the sheets could take your relationship to a whole new level since a touch of taboo is always a turn-on.

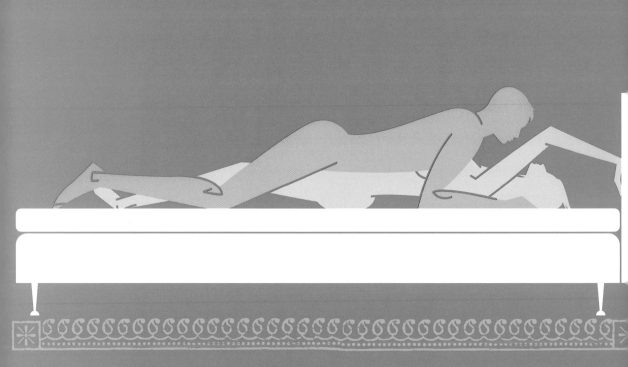

# Reach for the Heavens

### ■ Erotic Instructions:

Choose an immovable surface—a strong headboard or the side of a tub if you have a spacious bathroom. Lie on your back and raise your arms overhead so your palms rest flat on your surface of choice with your head several inches from the tub or the headboard; it's as if you're reaching for the sexual stars. Once he enters you missionary-style, bring your legs together as close as possible. With your thighs pressed tightly, his penis will rub against your inner thighs and labia each time he thrusts.

### ■ Why You'll Love It:

By holding yourself against that hard surface rather than moving with him, you create even more friction. Combined with your closed thighs, the immobility of this position makes for deeper penetration—a big plus for you. For him, the illusion of resistance will heighten his arousal.

**COSMO HINT**

Closing your thighs will stimulate your clitoris, resulting in an intense orgasm. But major friction can chafe dry skin, so make sure you're fully aroused. As far as he's concerned, the wetter the better, so moisten youself with lube for a truly slippery seduction.

# Sexual Seesaw

## ■ Erotic Instructions:

Do a few stretches before trying this one out! Lie on your back and lift your legs up and back until they land near your ears, parallel to the floor. Ask your man to kneel in front of you, with his knees against your lower back for support. Have him lean his torso against the underside of your thighs while you hold his legs to stay in this vixen-esque V-shape. After he enters you, slowly start to move in a seesaw motion.

## ■ Why You'll Love It:

Two things about this position will rock your world. First, raising your legs narrows your vaginal canal, making it a much tighter space and upping the intensity of his penetration. Second, spreading your legs for the Seesaw lets him plunge farther than ever. The pleasure-packed combination of the tantalizingly tight squeeze and the fabulous friction will send both of you soaring.

**COSMO HINT** Vary the pace and the intensity of the rocking. Just as one speed starts to feel unbelievable, switch it up. Go from slow to fast and back to slow again, drawing out the climax for as long as you can. Time it right, and you'll be headed for dual-orgasm delight.

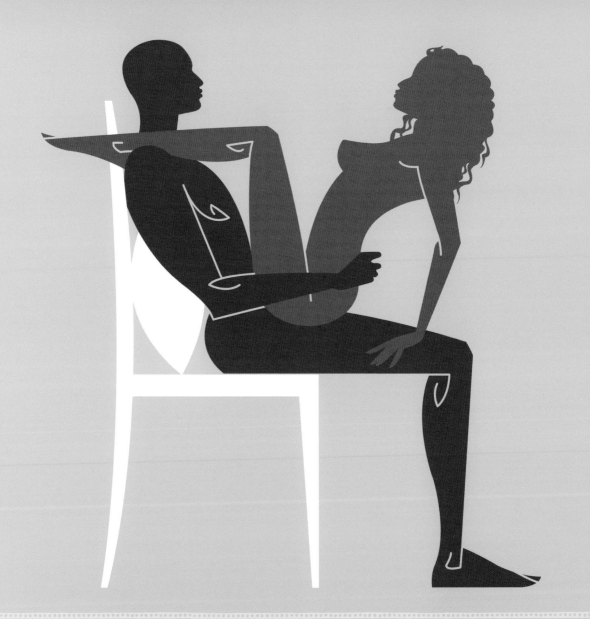

# Lap Dance

## ■ Erotic Instructions:

Find a tall-backed chair—such as one from your kitchen table or a desk—pad it with some pillows, and sit him down. Straddle his hardened member and lean back slightly, placing your hands on his knees. Extend your legs, one at a time, until each of your ankles is resting on one of his corresponding shoulders. Pump your booty back and forth at a speed that makes you moan. To supercharge your thrusting power, balance your weight between your ankles and your hands.

## ■ Why You'll Love It:

The Lap Dance has unmatched intimacy potential—how many people have seen you this close? This primo erotic view will give your guy fantasy material for weeks to come. Spice it up with some extra-special lingerie that you can seductively toss to turn him on to add even more steam to this sack session.

**COSMO HINT**

It doesn't take a pro to know that the best opening act for any lap dance is a sexy striptease. Put on a little mood music and slowly peel off your clothes. For an extra rush, tell him he can look but not touch—he'll be harder than ever by the time you mount him!

# Pinwheel

## ■ Erotic Instructions:

Both you and your man lie on your backs, with your bodies side by side but facing different directions (your head should be by his feet, and vice versa). Each of you should sit up halfway, relying on your elbows for support. Then move on top of your man, sliding down far enough so that he enters you comfortably. To gain some height, leverage your body off the ground with the help of your arms. Wrap your legs around either side of his torso. His legs should encircle your waist—one underneath your back, another on top of your stomach—and his hands grip your upper thighs as he starts to thrusts gently.

## ■ Why You'll Love It:

The Pinwheel will send you spinning more than any carnival ride! Like most side-by-side sex positions, this one promises ecstasy equality, but with a head-on twist. It's well suited for shallow penetrations. Your guy can tease the nerve endings in the first third of your vagina while also tantalizing the ultrasensitive head of his penis.

**COSMO HINT** To turbocharge his thrusting, try circling with your hips. The move doesn't have to be anything big—just enough to create a subtle spiral effect. If you're feeling really randy, move your body up and down his penis. The up-down, all-around action will be more than he can handle!

# Sensual Spoon

## Erotic Instructions:

Every couple knows how to assume the spoon: Lie on your side with your guy behind you. Keep both of your torsos in this doze pose and lift your top leg. Have him shift his lower body into a half-kneeling position, entering you from behind.

## Why You'll Love It:

This passion pose gives you the best of both worlds! The half-doggy-style, half-spooning hybrid combines the cozy intimacy of lying side by side with G-spot-rubbing penetration. Nothing beats having him holding you tight while taking you higher. Give him a gentle reminder that both his hands are free, guiding them to caress your curves and stimulate your clitoris. Up his ante by reaching behind, fondling his testicles, and stroking his perinium as he thrusts.

**COSMO HINT** It doesn't take much effort to get into this position, so try it out when he least expects it. After you two fall asleep spooning, wake your guy in the middle of the night and give it a whirl while you both are still half in dreamland. When you're done, fall back asleep with his arms wrapped snugly around you.

# Row His Boat

## ■ Erotic Instructions:

Find a comfortable but sturdy big chair. Ask your man to sit down, with his legs slightly spread. Face him and straddle his lap, keeping your knees bent and open against his chest. Brace your feet against the seat of the chair. While your guy grips your hips, thighs, or butt, you clutch the back of the chair and begin moving up and down along his shaft in a rowing motion.

## ■ Why You'll Love It:

There's no going gently down this stream. Row His Boat is all about the action, using the chair as a springboard. With your knees bent, use your hands and feet to make this the bounciest nooky style ever. It's perfect for teasing your guy with fast up-and-down action, then shifting gears and going for wide circular motions. Plus, your bodies are close enough for the intimacy of kissing, touching, or just giving each other incredibly lusty looks.

**COSMO HINT** The slicker, the better as you ride this wanton wave. Before you start bonking his buoy, grab a little extra lube to keep things extra wet. Heat things up more by putting your motion lotion on each other—the feel of your hands sliding against his most sensitve spots will definitely get him in the mood.

# SLOW DOWN HIS "O" AND SYNC UP

If you need to pull the emergency brake on your booty session, try one of these techniques to help him cool down while you can catch up.

| THE JERK | THE SQUEEZE | THE STOP AND GO |
|----------|-------------|-----------------|
| When his orgasm is just around the corner (he knows, and you might be able to feel his penis pulse and his body tighten up), gently hold his testicles and pull down slowly but firmly. This blocks the urethral passage and prevents ejaculation, giving you time to work your way to a worth-the-wait orgasm. | Wrap your thumb and index finger around the tip of his penis, under the ridge, and squeeze (gently) until he's no longer on the verge of orgasm. This move slows blood flow and temporarily dulls the sensation. In the meantime, work a little solo magic with your other hand to help you get closer to climax. | If he's on the edge and you're still climbing the mountain, stop stimulating him altogether. Instead, have him head downtown to give you hand (or mouth) action until you're able to get up to speed and he's cooled off. When you're just about there, have him enter you and head to the finish line together. |

*Source: Anne Hooper, Author of Sexopedia

# How to Find Your G-Spot

This elusive bliss button can trigger earth-shaking orgasms... and every woman has one. Here, the ABCs to locating your pleasure center.

## "What Is It, Exactly?"

The G-spot is a dime-size erogenous zone located just behind your front vaginal wall. When touched, it swells and brings on feelings of sexual bliss, similar to the way your clitoris responds to carnal contact. Most women say that when stroked it triggers powerful waves of pleasure.

## FEMALE EJACULATION?

A small percentage of women say that a G-spot induced orgasm triggers the release of a clear odorless liquid.

## "How Can I Find Mine?"

The simplest strategy: Insert your finger a few inches into your vagina, your palm facing up. Press into the front vaginal wall directly or make a come-hither "tickle" motion. "You should feel a spongy area about one-third of the way in," says Sandor Gardos, Ph.D., staff sexologist at mypleasure.com.

If your G is still in hiding, try searching for it from outside your body while your other hand is still inside. "Trace a line from your belly button to the top of your pubic bone, then press in and around the area," suggests Judy Kuriansky, Ph.D., a sex therapist in New York City and radio-show host. If you start to feel tingly, you've hit the spot.

When you do strike G-gold, don't be surprised if touching it makes you feel like you have to urinate. "Because of the proximity to the urethra, that gotta-go impulse is common and normal," says Hilda Hutcherson, M.D., associate professor of obstetrics and gynecology at Columbia University in New York City. After several seconds it'll be replaced by sensations of G-spot joy.

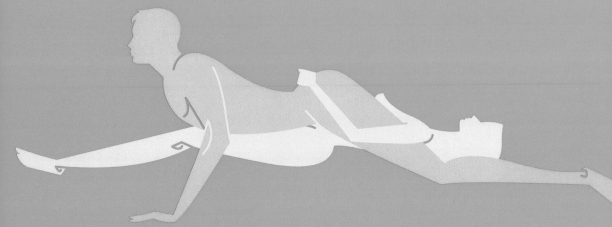

# Passion Propeller

## ■ Erotic Instructions:

Your man lies on top of you, entering you in traditional missionary style, but then—yowza!—he starts doing a 360-degree spin, all the while keeping his penis deep inside you. As he's rotating and thrusting, help guide him around your body the way a propeller would spin around the top of a helicopter. Make sure to lift his legs when they swing around over your head.

## ■ Why You'll Love It:

Once you make the jaw-dropping 360-degree journey, you and your man will feel like sexual dynamos and may even keep on spinning for rounds two, three, and four! Another plus of this topsy-turvy delight: As he's doing an around-your-world revolution, you finally get to view every inch of his body and barely have to move to reap big rewards—your propeller prince is doing all the work!

**COSMO HINT**

This randy ring around your rosie can make staying in sync tricky. If during his twisty travels you encounter some awkward private part match-up moments and it feels like he might just slip out, try placing a pillow under your butt to raise your pelvis a bit for easier access.

# Frisky Floor Show

## ■ Erotic Instructions:

Stand with your back to your man, then bend over slowly and put your palms on the floor. (If flexibility isn't your strong suit, simply bend your knees to adjust.) Have him enter you from behind, wrapping one of his arms around your waist so neither of you loses your balance. Should you start to go off kilter, press your hands firmly to the floor to steady yourself. If you want, grab some pillows for underneath your hands for extra support and comfort on your way to seventh heaven.

## ■ Why You'll Love It:

This position elevates your buttocks, allowing him to thrust downward at a unique angle. The internal pressure created by the force of his thrusting will stimulate your clitoris from the inside. Plus, the southern direction of his plunge will increase his chances of hitting your ultrasensitive G-spot.

**COSMO HINT** To double your naughty delight, try this moan-inducing move: While his member is pleasing your clitoris from the inside, have him reach around with his free hand and tend to your love button from the outside—the extra stimulation will absolutely floor you.

# Backup Boogie

## Erotic Instructions:

Your partner lies on his back, his legs straight out in front of him, a pillow under his head so he can watch the action. You straddle him with your head facing his feet. With your hands on the floor for support, you back up onto his penis. He holds your upper thighs or butt tightly while you thrust up and down the entire length of him.

## Why You'll Love It:

The Backup Boogie will become your first choice for doggy-style! You pick the angle and pace of the thrusting, so there's plenty of time and opportunity to experiment and find your inside hot spot. Get a rhythm down—circle for a few times before you take an unexpected plunge. It gives you maximum control for an intense orgasm, but your guy gets to savor every sensation without working up much of a sweat. And he'll love the total visual and tactile access to your wiggling backside.

**COSMO HINT**

If your knees get tired or start feeling sore, plant your feet and squat on top of him for a while. Changing positions like this will open up new angle and speed possibilities, and boost your erotic endurance, allowing you and your guy to go the extra mile.

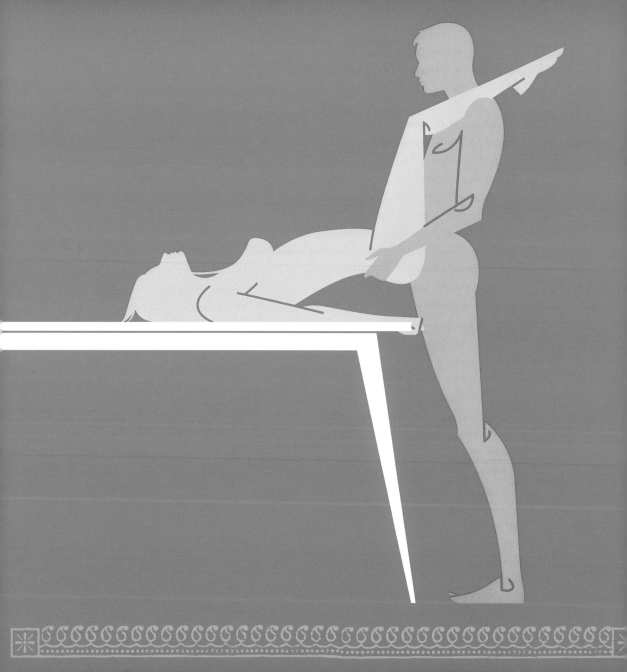

# Amazing Butterfly

## ■ Erotic Instructions:

The key to taking flight is lining up correctly with your lover. First, find a place where you can lie down and he can stand in front of you. The catch: It's got to be somewhere that puts your pelvis a foot lower than his—maybe your bed (if it's a high one) or a desk, counter, or even the hood of a car. Then lift your legs and rest them on his shoulders. Tilt your pelvis upward so that your back forms a straight line angling up toward him, and your crotches meet. Have him place his hands under your hips, so he can hold your booty at the perfect angle while he thrusts.

## ■ Why You'll Love It:

The Amazing Butterfly is primo for unequaled ecstasy without high-energy commitment. The pelvic tilt gives his penis full access to your vagina and builds in more fluttery friction for both of you. When done very slowly, it's completely dreamlike. The result? An orgasm that feels like you're flying.

**COSMO HINT** Add to your own personal pleasure with a little solo action. While you and your guy are going at it, use a free hand to stimulate your clitoris yourself. When your man sees you bringing on your own bliss, you'll send his desire flying.

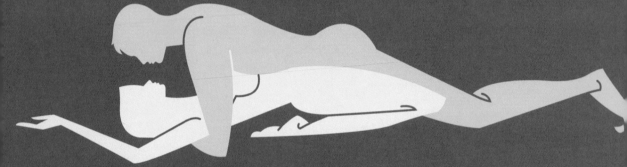

# Face-to-Face Fandango

## ■ Erotic Instructions:

This pose gives a whole new meaning to the words "Dirty Dancing." Lie on the floor or another flat surface faceup, with your legs bent under your thighs and your arms raised straight back over your head. Have your guy lie on top of you face-to-face, his legs straight and his hands gripping either your shoulders or your sides. Once you've tweaked the pose so that it's comfortable for you both, he can penetrate you with wide, circular motions or deep, up-and-down thrusting—whichever best suits your saucy mood.

## ■ Why You'll Love It:

Unlike other deep-access positions, this one allows for optimum eye contact, kissing, and touching. He can play with your breasts with his hands or tongue, and with your hands above your head, it's up to him to triple your trysting pleasure.

**COSMO HINT**

**With your legs bent under you and your arms straight over your head, your back will naturally be slightly arched. By bringing out your inner acrobat and arching even farther, you'll find that his member will reach even deeper delights.**

# The Erotic Roller Coaster

## ■ Erotic Instructions:

As your guy lies on his back, straddle him facing his feet. Sitting up straight with your hands on his hips, grind into him slowly for a few minutes, building up intense sensations. Think of the slow climb at the beginning of a roller coaster ride. Then, once you have the ideal angle, you can speed up, letting loose as you vary the depth of penetration. Next, lean back, steadying yourself with your hands (placed next to his sides) until your back presses against his chest. Then bring the racy ride back up again, and repeat until you're both fully thrilled. Whee!

## ■ Why You'll Love It:

Because there's little eye contact, your man feels free to engage in reckless role-playing, a major turn-on for you both. And when you lean back, he'll be able to caress your breasts, stomach, and clitoris, giving your hot bod the attention it deserves.

**COSMO HINT**

When you're in the sitting position, your hands will be free to do some randy roaming and play with his testicles. Give his hardware a couple of sensual strokes while you're starting. You'll have to stop when you lean back, but waiting for round two will have him hot and heavy, and begging for more.

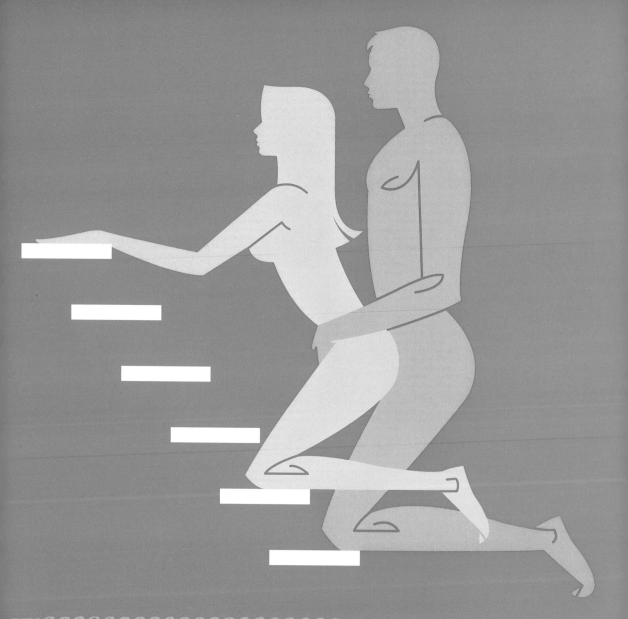

# Backstairs Boogaloo

## ■ Erotic Instructions:

Kneel in front of your partner at the landing of a staircase. Both of you should be facing the stairs, and your bodies should mesh together tightly. While you reach up and hold on to each side of the banister for support (or to the stairs themselves), he should hold your hips while he penetrates you from behind.

## ■ Why You'll Love It:

This mind-blowing pose lets your man use the incline of the staircase to enter you at a unique upward tilt, allowing him unlimited access to your G-spot. For more intense pressure, you can bear down on him so your butt meshes super snuggly with his groin—talk about a stairway to heaven!

**COSMO HINT**
Double your (and his) pleasure during this pose. If you hold on to the stairs with one hand and trigger your passion button with the other, the sensation is spine-tingling. When you can't take it anymore, reach through your legs to grope his testicles, sending the extra bliss his way.

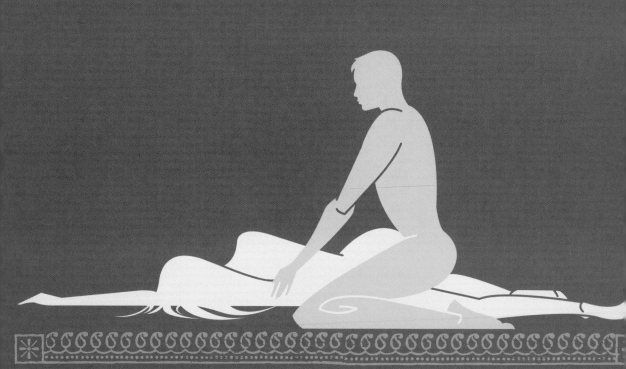

# The Boy's On-the-Side

## ■ Erotic Instructions:

With your back to your partner, lie down on your side. Have him kneel next to you on the bed facing toward your head, so your bodies are perpendicular. He slides the knee that's closer to you between your legs and then enters you. You take the leg that's on top and extend it out onto the bed, giving him a better view of your behind and the chance to hold on to your hips as he thrusts inside you.

## ■ Why You'll Love It:

With the Boy's On-the-Side, you can hit all those hard-to-reach spots. The unique angle of this sideways sex creates sensations that are sizzingly different from typical from-behind intercourse because it puts you in position to stimulate even the most tucked-away areas of your private parts.

**COSMO HINT**

To vary the sensation for you both, open your legs ever-so-slightly—just enough to give him access to your vagina. The closer together you keep them, the tighter you'll stay, and the more pleasing friction he'll feel on his member.

# Lap Limbo

## ▮ Erotic Instructions:

Your guy sits back in a roomy chair with a pillow placed under his knees to elevate them. Now you straddle him, lower yourself into his lap, and lean back so you're resting against his raised thighs. Bend your knees and put your legs over his shoulders so they rest on the back of the chair. He grasps your hips as he enters you, and you set the rocking in motion by pushing your feet against the top of the chair as he thrusts by pulling your hips toward him.

## ▮ Why You'll Love It:

The payoff of this racy recliner move starts with pure visual pleasure. With you in his lap, legs open, he's got an up-close-and-intimate view of you, plus easy access to touch your breasts, your tummy, and between your legs. All that tender stroking will intensify the sensual, superslow buildup brought on by his minimal movements.

**COSMO HINT**
Since you're in full control of the angle and depth of your stud's penetration in this position, you can aim his penis toward your navel to hit the G-spot. Be his tawdry tour guide and tilt your bod just the right way so he shares the feel-good sensations.

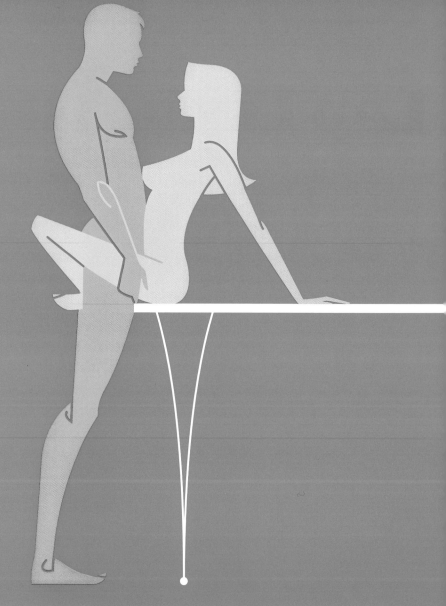

# Leg Lock

## ■ Erotic Instructions:

This one was made for the kitchen countertop. Hop up there and assume the spread-eagle position. With your man between your linked legs, have him thrust inside you. You'll be creating megaheat in a minimal amount of time.

## ■ Why You'll Love It:

Let's face it, sometimes you're not in the mood for languid, last-forever lovin'. Every now and then, you're so horny that you just want to orgasm—pronto! This move was made for those nights when you and your man can barely make it through the front door. There's no question you both will come quickly with this deeper-than-deep plunging. Plus, men get off on the novelty of doing it somewhere new—to them, out of the bedroom equals no-holds-barred sex.

**COSMO HINT** If you can't make it up the stairs to your apartment in time, try giving this a go right then and there on the steps. The best thing about the Leg Lock is its versatility—anywhere you can sit and he can stand will work just fine for you! Hmm, just imagine the possibilities.

# Joystick Joyride

## ◼ Erotic Instructions:

Your man lies on the bed or floor on his back with his arms relaxed above his head. Straddle him on top and slide your legs straight out and forward, so that your feet are on either side of his shoulders. Hold his shins or push on the floor for leverage, and start swiveling your hips in figure-eight motions so you're moving his penis around inside as you would the joystick of a video game.

## ◼ Why You'll Love It:

For the independent gal, this megamomentum move gives you tons of freedom and literally adds an exciting twist to your typical in–out motion. You control the speed, direction, and overall activity level. And as you're swiveling, your boobs will be bouncing north, south, east, and west—an exhibitionist's dream.

**COSMO HINT** Since you're calling the shots, tease and please him by suprising your game boy with unexpected hip twists: Vary your swivel with back-and-forth rubs, side-to-side fake-outs, and up-and-down dynamos. Not knowing what's coming next will make him feel like he's hit the high score.

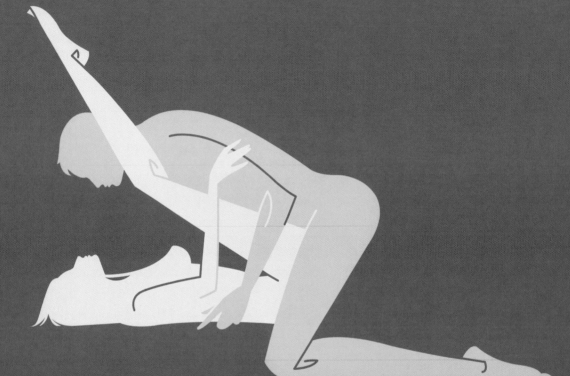

# The Rock 'n' Roll

## ■ Erotic Instructions:

Choose any flat surface—the floor or a bed, for instance—and lie faceup, bringing your knees up to your chin. He lies on top of you and while you rest your lower legs on his shoulders, your man should enter you just as he would in the missionary position. For some extra leverage, grab hold of his upper arms while he grips your hips and begins thrusting inside you.

## ■ Why You'll Love It:

This man-on-top position makes you feel deliciously open and vulnerable, while his incredibly deep thrusting drives you to superorgasmic heights. This is also a good position for extrasensual couples who enjoy a little lip action when they're knocking boots. Since you're face-to-face, it's easy for him to give into his primal urges and lick, suck, or nibble on your mouth while you're rocking each other's worlds.

**COSMO HINT** Once you've set a steady pace and feel comfortable enough to hang on to him with just one hand, use the other to stroke his shoulders, back and chest. The sensory combination of seeing your hot bod underneath him and feeling new sensations will send him into overdrive.

# Supersize Your Sutra

To really elevate your bliss to cloud-nine sublime, add one—or heck, try all—of these erotic extras.

 **Bedeck Your Bed**

Indulge in superluxe, high thread-count sheets. But be sure to stay away from flannels or else you and your man will find yourselves sweating Sahara-style.

 **Slick Up**

A Kama Sutra lust session requires lots of energy, so rub lavender, mint, or lemon-scented oil on your body before you get down to business—it will give you an invigorating lift and keep you from sticking to your stud. And your sexy scent will linger on your linens, so you can bet he'll be craving you later.

 **Enrich Your Kissing**

Try these Kama-tized lip-locks: Gently suck on your man's upper lip while he kisses your lower one, then take both of your guy's lips between yours. Or caress his lips with two fingers, lightly lick them with your tongue, then press deeply into his mouth.

**Meld With Music**

Nothing sets the mood for love and lust quite like slow sensual music. So choose a CD by an artist you and your man both love. Or, we suggest popping in a sultry Indian music CD with scales and rhythms called raggas, which are said to spark sensual emotions and heighten sexual feelings.

 **Breathe Deeply**

It may sound fairly obvious, but in the heat of passion, people often take such shallow breaths that they quickly lose steam. Instead, open your mouth, loosen your jaw, and take big belly breaths as you're thrusting—it will help you build toward orgasm. Plus, all that hot and heavy huffing and puffing is a surefire way to let him know how totally into it you are. For him, there's no greater turn on.

# MOOD MAKER VS. DEAL BREAKERS

There's a fine line between totally erotic… and just plain idiotic.

| MAKER | BREAKER |
|---|---|
| A couple of small candles around your bed | A hundred candles around your bed like an altar |
| Barry White on the CD player | Barry Manilow on the tape deck |
| A glass of vintage wine | A box of vintage wine |
| Dressing up like a nurse | Dressing up lika a nun |
| Whispering in his ear, "I want you now." | Screaming at the top of your lungs, "Do me now!" |
| A baby-doll nightie | A granny gown |
| Taking a shower together | Shaving your legs while he's trying to soap your back |

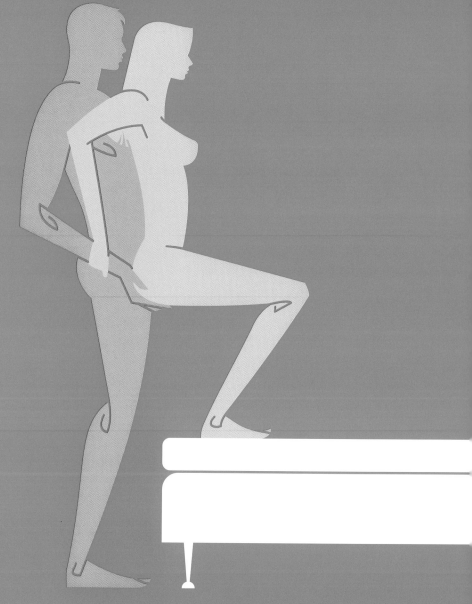

# Lusty Lean

## ■ Erotic Instructions:

Climb up on the bed or a chair with your back to him and squat down. Have him stand behind you, so your shoulders are against his chest. Lean on him as he steadies you by placing his hands on your hips or under your rear. When he enters you, adjust the width of your legs to allow him to go deeper. Think of your knees as little springs and enhance his thrusting with your own little moves.

## ■ Why You'll Love It:

Leaning back on his chest and bracing yourself on his biceps, you'll feel totally taken care of—and he'll feel more studly than a first-string stallion. Plus, gravity is on your side, giving him hot, deep access combined with more of a grinding motion than the usual from-behind fast thrusting.

**COSMO HINT**
Once you have the rhythm down, change it up a little. So long as he can support you in his weakened state, have him take half a step back. Changing the angle will alter where his penis hits your vaginal walls, enhancing your climax by drawing it out.

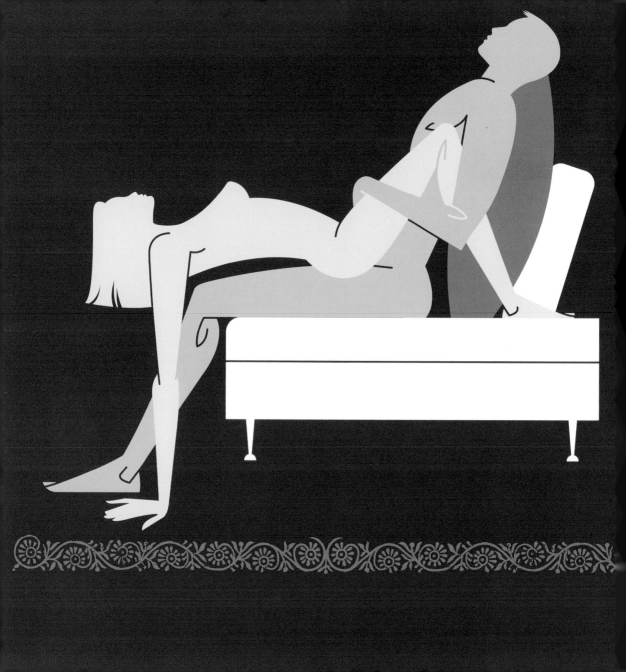

# Couch Canoodle

## ■ Erotic Instructions:

Have your partner sit back on a couch (or a comfy chair). Straddle his lap with your legs splayed apart and your knees bent up against his chest. Slowly lean back so you're almost upside down with your arms stretched behind you (all the way to the floor) to support your weight and maintain your balance. Thrust back and forth against him, opening and closing your legs.

## ■ Why You'll Love It:

This passion pose supplies the kind of naughty sex scene that all men yearn for. It gives him a full-frontal va-va-voom view of you in action, one that'll undoubtedly fuel his dirtiest fantasies for a long, long time. Plus, because you're the one who sets the speed and timing, you can treat yourself to the exact motions that make you moan with desire and take you over the edge of ecstasy.

**COSMO HINT**

Take advantage of being on top by clamping your PC muscles around him, transforming your privates into the tight space he craves. When you're ready for him to hit his peak, squeeze your PC muscles extra hard, or pulse them, and the move is bound to send him soaring.

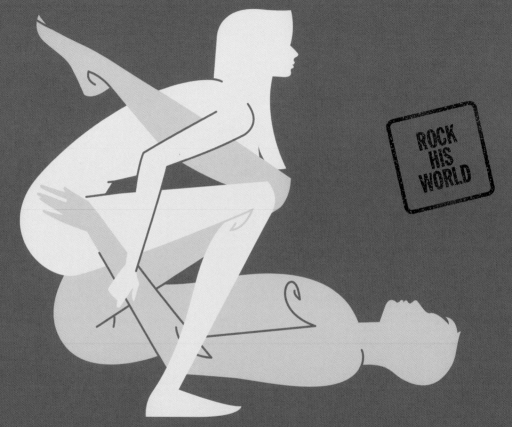

ROCK
HIS
WORLD

# Erotic Accordion

## ■ Erotic Instructions:

Have your man lie on his back and lift his knees toward his chest. Facing him, straddle his hips and squat down, so your thighs are hugging his. Lower yourself onto him—the closer he draws his knees to his chest, the better access you'll have to his member. You're in control here, so bend at your knees and move up and down.

## ■ Why You'll Love It:

For babes who like to mix up their mattress sessions with a tawdry twist, this sexy pose will give you power and allow him to show his submissive side. Plus, the sensitive outer banks of your vagina and the nerve-rich head of his main attraction will be delighted by the shallow penetration. Trust us, you and your partner will be making sweet music together in no time!

**COSMO HINT**

Before you start, agree to keep your eyes open and your gazes locked. Since you're directly facing each other, you and your guy will both get a prime panorama of each other's ecstatic expressions. Those red-hot glances will instantly arouse his most base desires.

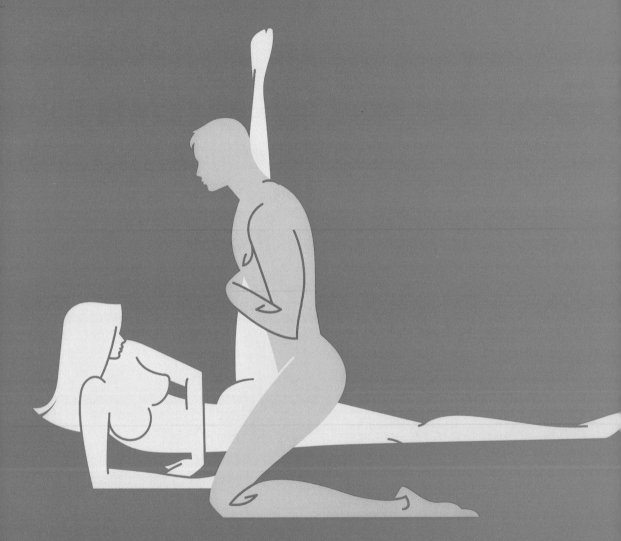

# Romp with a View

## ■ Erotic Instructions:

Lie on your side on a sturdy surface (if you opt for the bed, make it first—the tangled sheets will only get in the way with this pose) with one arm propping up your head or bent under your body for support. Keeping one leg stretched out along the bed or floor, extend the other straight up in the air so it's perpendicular to your body. Your partner can then straddle your grounded leg and enter you while holding your other leg up or letting it rest against his shoulder for leverage, whichever happens to satisfy his passion preference.

## ■ Why You'll Love It:

With your leg against his bod, your man can use it to leverage himself into the hottest pose possible. And he can penetrate you in up-and-down motions instead of regular back-and-forth thrusting. The different strokes will bring on ultrasensual new sensations.

**COSMO HINT** With your free hand, reach up and run your fingers across his chest as you gaze longingly into his eyes. Then, slowly, carefully stroke his nipples which is a major turn-on for lots of guys.

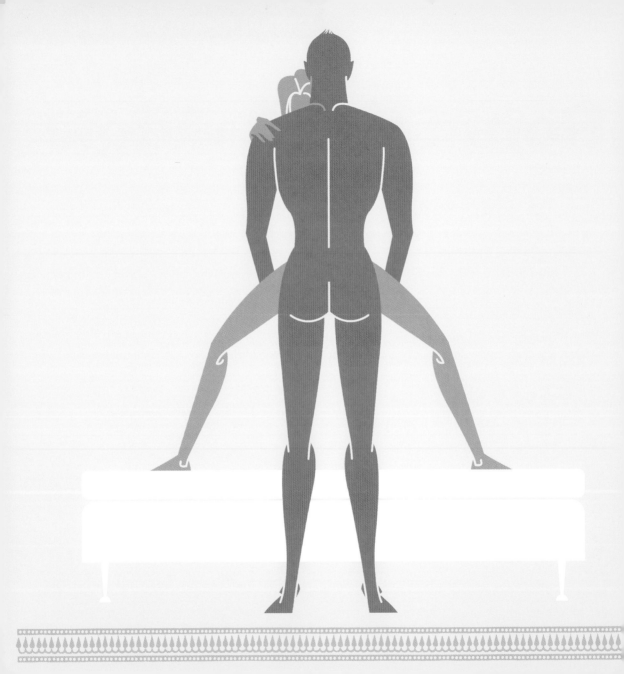

# Sofa Spread-Eagle

## Erotic Instructions:

Stand on the edge of a couch, bed, or two chairs, with your legs spread wide. Position your man so he's standing on the floor facing you. Adjust the width of your stance (bending your knees slightly if necessary) so he can easily slide between them and get your pelvises to meet—then rock your bodies together to feel the bliss.

## Why You'll Love It:

There's nothing like the feeling of impulsive, must-have-it-right-now sex while standing up. But the Sofa Spread-Eagle spares you both the royal pain of matching up your private parts. While your stable stance allows you to move to his rhythm, your wide-spread legs give you that supersexy vulnerable feeling. All that frontal friction will hit your hot spot and take you to a no-hands-necessary climax.

**COSMO HINT**

Because you are both standing, nothing should hold you back! Get in some hands-on action—whether you're stroking the back of his neck or tickling his testicles, he'll love the attention. Ensure you're satisfied by guiding his lips to your breasts and placing his fingers where you want them.

# Sexy Scissor

## ■ Erotic Instructions:

You lie faceup on a desk or tabletop with your hips perched on the very edge. Raise your legs toward the ceiling so they're at an eye-popping ninety-degree angle from your torso, then have your guy grab your ankles. He extends his arms out to his sides, and as your legs are spread-eagled, he enters you while standing. Next, he starts alternately crossing and spreading your legs like scissors, opening and closing as he thrusts.

## ■ Why You'll Love It:

No other love lock will offer you such a body-rockin' range of sensations. One second your limbs are in an erotic X and you're supertight for a snug fit—then suddenly you're wide open and able to take him in deliciously deep. We guarantee these thigh-melting maneuvers will lead to mucho bliss.

**COSMO HINT**

Since your hands are totally free to roam, you can give him one hell of a show by sensually caressing your breasts. Or give yourself a hand and stroke your clitoris to add yet another mind-melting sensation to the already bliss-inducing mix.

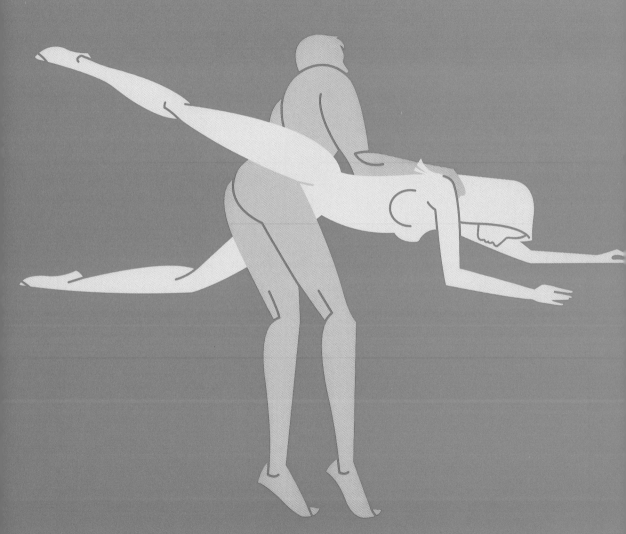

# Carnal Crisscross

## ■ Erotic Instructions:

Start by lying on your side with your arms above your head. With your man on his side and his body perpendicular to yours, slowly raise your top leg and let him inch his lower body between your legs. Once you're joined at the groin, have him grab your shoulders while you anchor yourself on the floor. Both of you will need to hold on tight for this stellar trip!

## ■ Why You'll Love It:

This sideways sex position is one for the record books! On top of the typical thrusting, you two can enjoy some serious shallow grinding. Plus, this new entry angle allows him to explore every inch of your inner sanctum, especially the oft-ignored sides, providing you with an array of lusty sensations.

**COSMO HINT**

Go over the top by twisting your torso as he thrusts deeper. Think mini corkscrew: If your stomach is facing the floor, tilt back ever-so-slightly; if your back is angling toward the bed, turn forward a little. It won't take much to send him flying.

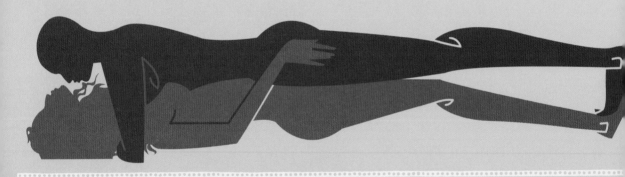

# The Soft Rock

## ■ Erotic Instructions:

Try this tantalizing twist on the typical missionary position (him on top, you on bottom). Instead of having your man rest on his elbows, ask him to slide two to four inches forward. Have him place his arms on either side of your shoulders, letting his body fall flat against yours. Make sure you both keep your spines straight. With your legs touching his, push your pelvis up about two inches. Your man should push down gently, providing a little counter-resistance. Instead of the usual in-and-out of thrusting, rock up and down.

## ■ Why You'll Love It:

Okay, so missionary doesn't always make you quake. But because he's in a more forward position, the base of his penis should naturally rub your clitoris. The rocking motion draws out the orgasm, building pleasure gradually. Because both sets of genitals are sharing such tight quarters, your climb to the climax will be intensified.

**COSMO HINT**
To add extra oomph to this passion pose, give his cheeks a firm squeeze, then trail your fingers slowly up his back. When you reach his head gently run your fingers over his scalp then pull him in for a kiss he'll never forget.

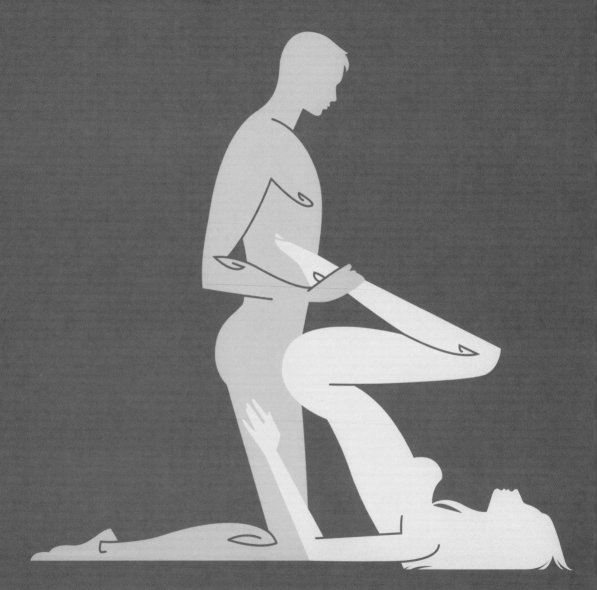

# The G-Force

## ■ Erotic Instructions:

Lie down on your back and pull your knees close to your chest. Ask your guy to kneel in front of you, grabbing hold of your feet with his hands. Have him penetrate you, thrusting forward from his hips. Looking to add even more God-that's-good action? Put your feet on his chest and have him hold on to your hips—it'll give him extra control and let him plunge even farther.

## ■ Why You'll Love It:

You have to hand over the reins to him, but it's worth it. For those who know the power of the G-spot, the deep, intense penetration will send you spinning. And there's no reason he can't be doing double duty. The G-Force is the perfect position for him to be inside you while using his hand to stimulate your clitoris. If you can surrender your on-top status, this is one position where the Force will be with you.

**COSMO HINT**

To keep him excited while he's at work, give him a little visual perk. He's perfectly positioned to watch your reactions, so don't hold back with your facial expressions. Make sure you show him exactly how much you appreciate his multitasking.

# The Wow-Him Powwow

## ■ Erotic Instructions:

Sit your man down with his legs crossed. Facing him, straddle his legs and lower yourself into his lap—without him penetrating you. Wrap your legs around either side of his torso, so they're hugging his buttocks. Then, as you hold each other's arms or lower backs tightly, he enters you. Start to slowly rock back and forth together, increasing your speed as you come closer to climaxing.

## ■ Why You'll Love It:

Like the standard missionary position, this takes eye contact and body-to-body closeness to the max but adds a passion perk. The comfy upright pose encourages equal control over the speed and timing of his thrusting, allowing for a gradual build-up of pleasure for both partners. Plus, your clitoris is at an easy-to-reach angle, allowing him to stroke your love button without interrupting the hot-and-heavy action.

**COSMO HINT** Vary your rocking to prolong the pleasure. You can grind into each other slowly, then suddenly speed up or get deep, then tease each other with shallow penetrations. Get creative—you never know what combo will wow you both to bliss.

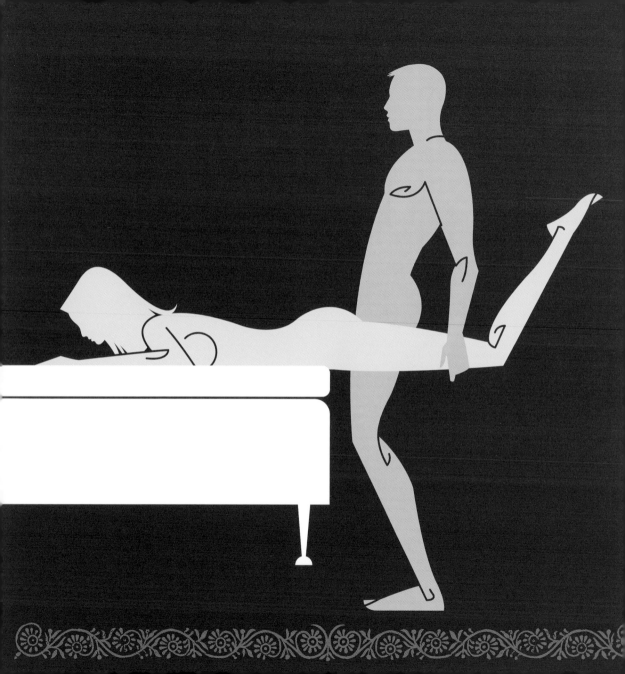

# Bed Spread

## ■ Erotic Instructions:

Bend over the side of the bed so your stomach and breasts are against the mattress and your feet are on the floor, legs spread comfortably. As your guy penetrates you from behind, he lifts your legs from just above the knees, holds them apart, and thrusts.

## ■ Why You'll Love It:

With your body angled slightly downward and your legs apart, he gets deep penetration. And since your gams are in his grip, he can thrust away with total abandon. Plus, he can easily view your sexy rear and watch himself move in and out of you—an up close and personal pose guys pine for. So what's in it for you? You feel weightless with your legs lifted off the floor, as if you're floating, while your guy does all the work. And his penis is perfectly angled for your pleasure.

**COSMO HINT**

When your man is getting close to climaxing, urge him to shift his hands from your legs to your hips. This sudden but subtle adjustment will make for an extra-frisky finale as he gains even more control.

# THE PERFECT POSITION FOR YOU

If you and your man need help meshing, here's how to pick the perfect pose for any mismatch woe.

| THE PROBLEM | THE SOLUTION | WHY IT WORKS |
| --- | --- | --- |
| He climaxes before you do. | The Erotic Accordion | The shallow penetration helps him keep a lid on it. |
| You climax before he does. | The Head Game | His take-charge thrusts will speed his ascent to seventh heaven. |
| His penis is plus-size. | The Randy Recliner | You control the depth. |
| He has a short stack. | The Sexual Seesaw | It narrows your canal. |
| He weighs more than you. | The Wanton Wheelbarrow | You bypass his belly entirely. |
| You're bigger than he is. | The Sensual Spoon | You're both on your sides so he won't carry your weight. |

# Sizzling Sex Sampler

Stuck in a one-note nooky rut? Here, mix-and-match your mattress menus to satisfy your every carnal craving.

## Stoke Your Love Fire

**Renew your wows with these heart-to-heart dishes.**

 **APPETIZER** You Under Him (Reach For the Heavens) Get head-to-toe in touch with each other.

 **MAIN COURSE** Side by Side (Now and Zen) Enjoy intense eye contact and blissful body rubbing.

 **DESSERT** Amazing Butterfly. Just when you thought you couldn't fall any more deeply... you do.

## Make It a Kinky Lite Night

**Feed your hunger for over-the-edge ecstasy.**

 **APPETIZER** You on Top (Straddle His Saddle) Start things off right with a twist-and-shout bout.

 **MAIN COURSE** Doggy Style (G-Spot Jiggy) Set your inner bad girl free and you'll feel oh so-o-o good.

 **DESSERT** You Sitting, Him Standing (Leg Lock) Blow him away with a built-for-him bang.

## Quench a Doing-It Drought

**Release your pent-up passion by taking fast action.**

 **APPETIZER** You both Standing (Pleasure Pick-Me-Up) Bring him over the brink in a blink.

**MAIN COURSE** You in charge (Joystick Joyride) Unleash your pent-up passion with this decadent pose.

 **DESSERT** Bonded together (Spider Web) Have a sweet, slow, simultaneous second helping of each other.

# Stand and Deliver

## ■ Erotic Instructions:

Stand against a wall with your legs slightly spread. Have your man face you, grab the backs of your thighs, and carefully lift you up (you should be high enough so that your legs rest against his hips). You can help him by pushing your back into the wall for leverage. Put your hands on his shoulders or your arms around his neck for balance. He thrusts away, keeping his knees bent and pushing from his hips.

## ■ Why You'll Love It:

The Stand and Deliver fulfills two sex cravings in one oh-my-God move. First off, it satisfies your up-close-and-personal need for face-to-face intimacy. But stand-up sex also scratches that take-me itch that consumes passionate partners. This position is primal and versatile—perfect for fast satisfaction.

**COSMO HINT**
When you two are well on your way to the Big O, add intensity by squeezing your thighs a little bit tighter. The extra tension will narrow your vaginal canal, which in turn enhances the friction he feels. Plus, clenching your muscles creates more tension in your body, and thus more pleasure build-up.

# The Linguini

## ▉ Erotic Instructions:

Lie on your side, putting a pillow under your head for extra support. Your man kneels directly behind your butt, leaning ever-so-slightly over your body. He should push one of his knees between your legs, positioning his body so he can penetrate you. He places one hand on your back to help support himself as he goes for the plunge. The key to your pleasure is keeping your limbs as limp as a noodle.

## ▉ Why You'll Love It:

This side-by-side canoodle creates incredible friction for him because your thighs are so close together. Plus, having your thigh curved at that angle gives him deeper access. The combo of these two will make even the tiniest guy feel like a god! And while he teases your G-spot, he can nuzzle your breasts or reach around and play with your clitoris—covering all the pleasure bases.

**COSMO HINT**

Right before he reaches the point of no return, plant your feet on the bed and push your body away. Slipping his penis out for even a nanosecond will disrupt the action and draw out your pleasure. An added bonus? You get to relive that give-me-more feeling of him entering you for the first time.

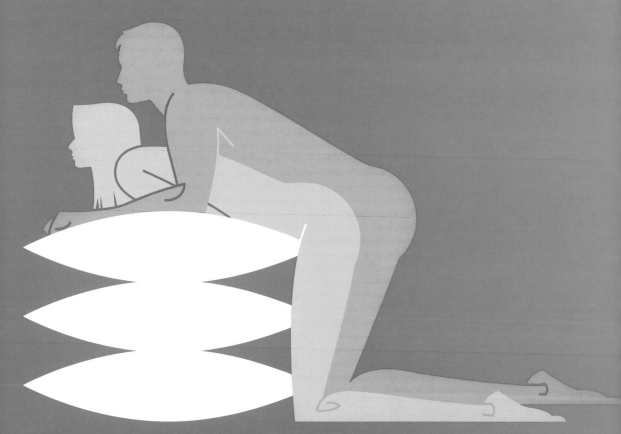

# Magic Mountain

## ■ Erotic Instructions:

Arrange a big pile of pillows on the floor and relax into it face-first, following its mountain shape so your back naturally arches. Your man lies on top of you with both of you facing in the same direction, his chest glued to your back and his arms over yours. Using the pillows for support, open your legs so he can kneel between them and enter you from behind.

## ■ Why You'll Love It:

He gets the mischievous thrill of doing it doggy-style, a position every lover boy goes gaga for, but with supersoft support for you both. With all that padding beneath you, he can go all-out wild with the thrusting. And unlike most backside boinks, his whole upper body is one with yours, giving intimacy addicts an ultrasensual head-to-toe connection. Focus on this skin-to-skin contact to add yet another sensation to the mix.

**COSMO HINT** Switch around your body positions to have even more fun on the mountain of lust. Climb a little higher so that he's almost lying on top of you for a while, then descend a bit so you're practically sitting in his lap. Each tweak will give you something new to moan about.

# Sideways Samba

## ■ Erotic Instructions:

You lie on your side on the bed or floor, turned away from your guy with your legs straight out in front of you at a ninety-degree angle to your torso (so you make an L-shape). Your guy lies behind you on his side in a modified spoon position, lines up his genitals with yours, then raises his torso with his arms, placing his topmost hand on the other side of your body next to your chest. Entering you, he controls the motion as he moves in and out of you.

## ■ Why You'll Love It:

If your man's member is more petite than plus-sized, this one's for you. At this angle, he can give you maximum penetration. Plus, the skewed point of entry means his lusty limb hits all sides of your vagina (not just the top and bottom), giving you tons of sizzling sensations and a fiery finale.

**COSMO HINT**

Use lube. If you keep your legs pressed together, you'll create a serious friction fest, which means more stimulation for both of you. But you'll definitely need to keep things slippery so he can easily slip and slide in and out.

THE
PERFECT
QUICKIE
POSITION

# Hang Ten

## ■ Erotic Instructions:

While standing up, bend forward with your legs spread slightly, your back straight, and your hands resting on your knees for balance. Your guy enters you from behind, pulling himself as close to you as possible while holding your torso for support. Have him bring you even closer until your bodies come into full contact. He leans slightly over you to gain pumping power.

## ■ Why You'll Love It:

This hang-over pose is excellent for that need for fast, frenzied sex. Being bent forward gives your guy maximum depth and control, and the angle allows for incredible pleasure. Since his hands are wrapped around your body, he'll be itching to wander over your breasts, hips, tummy, and thighs. And unlike typical from-behind positions that can leave you feeling disconnected from your dude, your lower torsos and legs are always touching—making the position feel secure and intimate.

**COSMO HINT** Urge him to stay still while you grind your behind in circles; the sudden sensation alteration will take your breath away. When he starts up again, you slow it down for a while—with both of you moving, it could easily get too hot to handle. Then again, maybe that's the goal.

# Spider Web

## ■ Erotic Instructions:

Both you and your guy lie on your sides, facing each other. Lean in close together and scissor your legs through his so you're superclose and he's deep inside you as he enters you. While thrusting, hold on to each other for leverage and ultimate friction.

## ■ Why You'll Love It:

Rather than typical in-and-out thrusting, this sexual web your bodies create lets you and your guy please each other with grinding, circular motions. Try gyrating your hips in circles around his member for an incredible erotic explosion. It's a tight-together fit that generates lots of tension, yet lets you kiss, nibble, and stroke each other while doing the deed. You can reach behind and rake your nails lightly along his back, causing spine-tingling sexy shivers—a major erotic move he may not expect, but one that will make him moan even more.

**COSMO HINT** Let your fingers venture even further south and surprise him by reaching back and stroking his perineum, the area below his anus that's rich in nerve endings. But make sure you're just about to reach *your* peak, because this move is sure to speed up his arrival of the Big O.

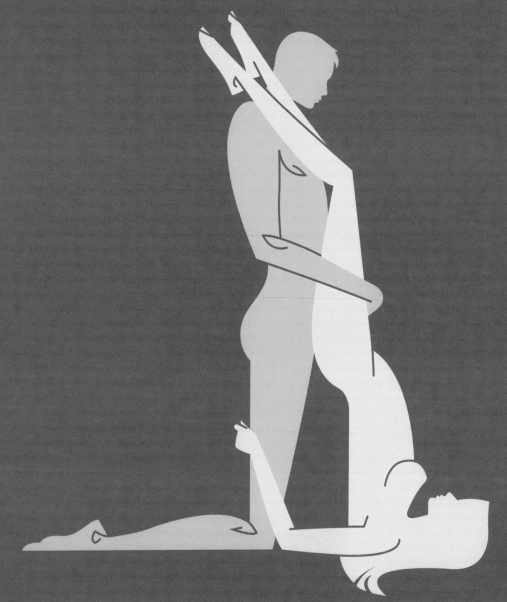

# Head Game

## ■ Erotic Instructions:

Start this inverted delight by lying flat on the ground face up. With your hands supporting your lower back, lift your legs and backside way, way up so they're as perpendicular to the ground as you can get them. Have your man kneel before you, grab your ankles, and bring his knees to your shoulders. Then take his hands and ask him to hold your hips—that will steady you both. Hold his thighs for leverage and adjust so your genitals can join for some otherworldly upside-down action.

## ■ Why You'll Love It:

Getting into this position, you may feel like you're headed nowhere—but it's totally worth it once you experience the results. The blood rush from your thighs will intensify the sensations in the pelvic region. Plus, your legs are squeezed together over his shoulders, which guarantees a snug, scintillating fit for him.

**COSMO HINT**

Once you two are well on your way, pulse your legs ever-so-slightly. The added thigh movement will give him an extra rush in this already tight fit. Thrust your hips into his groin and arch your back as you move with him, turning you into a vibrating vixen he can't resist.

# The Dragon

## ■ Erotic Instructions:

Lie on your stomach with your arms raised above your head. With a pillow or two placed under your pubic bone, spread your legs slightly. Have your partner stretch his body over yours and enter you, mimicking the position that you're in. Instead of fast from-behind thrusting, this steamy stance requires a circular, swirling motion.

## ■ Why You'll Love It:

The circular stimulation will slowly electrify your entire vagina, bringing on a subtle yet superstrong orgasm. There isn't a lot of motion with this position, so it's a good one to try if he's prone to come quickly and you want to delay his climax (or if you just want to savor the feel of each other's bodies). Ask him to explore the more neglected parts of your body like your back and the base of your neck with his lips, tongue, and even his teeth. This him-on-top is all about you, you, you.

**COSMO HINT** Even though you're not on top, you can still be a major player in this pose. If you match the speed of his sensual swirling with your hips, your bodies will move as one big, undulating sexual monster. Speed up or slow down together to maintain the momentum.

FOR STUDS
SEEKING
A NEW
SENSATION

# Supernova

## ■ Erotic Instructions:

Begin in the deceptively down-to-earth woman-on-top position on a made bed. (Don't get under the covers.) But instead of riding him with his body lengthwise on the mattress, mount your man as he lies perpendicular to the pillows—you'll see why in a second. Once you're climbing toward climax, stop moving and gently grab the sides of his torso with your hands. Leaning on your knees, inch him toward the edge of the bed until his head, shoulders, and arms hang backward over the side. Then start riding him again.

## ■ Why You'll Love It:

You're in complete control here, and the reason it feels so good is that you're literally sitting on his member, giving him no choice but to bury himself deep inside you. And when he's upside down, the blood will rush to his head, allowing him to experience what's called erotic inversion, and sending tingles to his upper body that will turn his climax into an otherworldly experience.

**COSMO HINT**

While he's at your mercy, treat your guy to this triple-his-pleasure move: Lick your fingers and swirl them around his pecs, moving inward until you reach his nipples, then give each a gentle pinch.

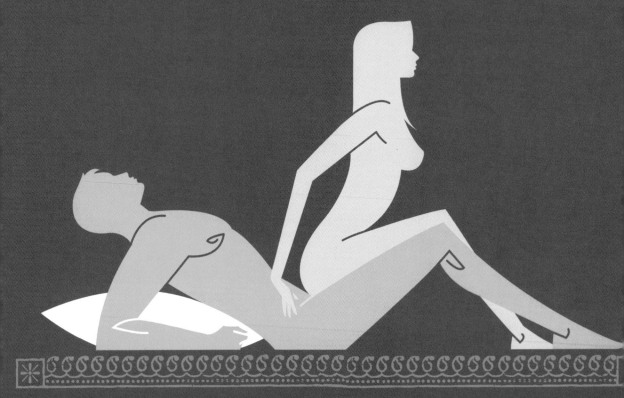

# Love Seat

## ■ Erotic Instructions:

Tell your partner to lie back, propping up his head and shoulders with a pillow, and have him spread his legs slightly. While you're facing the same direction—your back is to his face—lower yourself onto his hardened penis. Put your feet between his legs on the floor or the bed. Take your right hand and place it on his right hip bone and your left hand on the bed next to his left hip bone. Use your hands and feet to move your body up and down on his shaft.

## ■ Why You'll Love It:

The movement of *your* seat is the key to the Love Seat. With both your hands and feet controlling your motion, ride your behind up and down at a pace that feels best. While you're doing all the work, give your man's hands a pleasure project and have him massage your butt, back, neck, and other sexy spots he doesn't always have access to.

**COSMO HINT**

Feeling but not seeing your partner lets you experiment with a fantasy or two. Give yourself momentary permission to pretend he's Brad Pitt, Tom Cruise, or a total stranger. A Cosmo word of caution: Just be sure you're calling out the right guy's name!

# Tight Squeeze

## ■ Erotic Instructions:

Lie down on your stomach and, keeping your legs straight, spread them slightly. Rest your arms by your side, or stretch them out in front of you. Have your guy stretch his body over yours, resting on his elbows so he doesn't place all his weight on you. He then positions his legs outside your legs. As he enters you, close your legs and cross them at the ankles.

## ■ Why You'll Love It:

With your legs clenched and your ankles crossed, you can feel the entire length of your man's member and grip it tight, creating loads of feel-good friction as he thrusts deep. While you're rocking randily, have him reach under you and play with your breasts, or brush his lips against your neck and nibble on your earlobe. Though this move offers megasensation, there isn't a lot of motion, so it's a prime pose for guys hoping to hold off on climaxing.

**COSMO HINT** Get the full benefit of the intense carnal contact and really savor the weight of his body, the feel of his chest, legs, arms, breath . . . To make this connection even steamier, pump your booty back and forth into his hips as he's thrusting for some dual action.

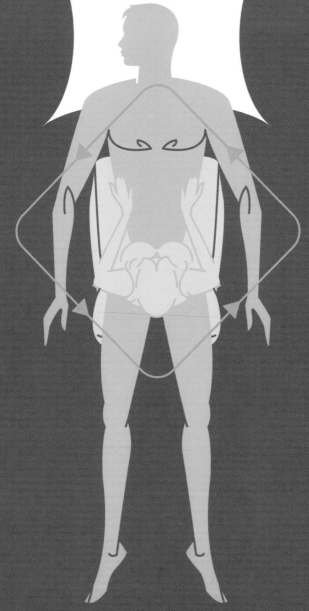

# Diamond in the Buff

## ■ Erotic Instructions:

Have your guy lie on his back, and prop a pillow under his head. Facing him, straddle his pelvis and lower yourself onto his member, placing your hands and knees on either side of his torso. Now here's the sensational jewel of this position: Once he's deep inside you, gently move in the diagonal shape of a diamond: to the left, then up, right, and down.

## ■ Why You'll Love It:

The reason this feels so good is that your man's penis glides against every steamy inch of you. Not only can you take him in all the way, but he gets to have all sides of his member massaged, too. And since the slow, controlled motions won't wear you out the way fast up-and-down thrusts can, you two will enjoy a long session of intense face-to-face intimate action.

**COSMO HINT**

To really make this move shine, you can easily set his penis to hit your G-spot—by scooching your sexy body into the "down" position, or what would be the bottom of the dirty diamond. You may need to shift your hips around to locate the exact lusty spot.

# Your N-Zone

Nipples: two hot buttons that provide mucho pleasure.

Sure, they'll come in handy when you need to nurse your babies one day, but the only purpose nipples seem to serve in the pre-mommy years is providing an instant weather update to everyone in sight. Most guys, in fact, tend to rush past the "N-Spot" on their way to the ultimate goal. But your nipples are acutally pleasure buttons, capable of priming you for passion. Here, the secret to nipple nirvana.

## A Pointers Primer

A nipple consists of two parts- the tip and the areola. Both areas are packed with supersensitive nerve endings. But what's even more amazing is that "there's a direct connection between the nerves in your nipples and your clitoris," explains Michael Ra Bouchard, Ph.D., clinical sexologist and director of the Aloha Sexual Health and Happiness Center in Maui, Hawaii. That's why the right stroke or squeeze leaves you tingling down below.

## Give Him a Hand

Guide your man's hand to one of your twin peaks and experiment with different types of touch, like circling your nipple with one fingertip or lightly squeezing it while varying the pressure to keep you on the erotic edge. Once your man has you worked into a frenzy, ask him to brush an ice cube against each nipple. The cold will further boost your sensitivity.

## Get Tongue-Tied

Now, triple your nipple pleasure with some oral attention. He might try gently biting or playfully pulling on them with his lips. You can also suggest that he slowly lick your areolae with the flat of his tongue, as he would an ice-cream cone. And if he's ready to multitask, have him suck one nipple while using his hand to tantalize you below the belt.

## NIP TIDBIT

Almost 1 percent of women are actually able to reach orgasm just by having their nipples stimulated.

# HIS V-ZONE

Think you know every erotic inch of his body? We discovered a new moan zone you might be neglecting...

### TAKE A LOOK

Eye your man's below-the-belt region. If you start at each hip bone and draw two lines diagonally down, meeting between his legs, you'll see it forms a V-shape. Well, in those crevices (where thigh meets pelvis) are ligaments that are surrounded by nerve endings. The skin here is also thin, so it's very sensitive.

### USE YOUR FINGERS

Using the tips of your index and middle fingers, caress both hollows at the same time to get his motor running.

### GET ORAL

You can also turn him on orally. Sensuously kiss and lick along each line. It gives him a tickling sensation that'll travel to his genitals. Plus, as you're exploring with your mouth, your cheek will be grazing his manhood—a delicious tease that'll have him and you aching for more. But don't give into your desires too soon! Remember—the longer you hold off from doing the deed, the more anticipation will build and the more mind-blowing it will be.

## TABOO TERRITORY?

Many men like to have their back-door region stimulated, but they don't often admit it since it's considered kind of kinky. To test your guy's comfort level, try caressing his butt cheeks and then slowly inching inward. He'll let you know if it's a go or a no-no.

GET
CLOSER
THAN EVER
BEFORE

# Arc de Triomph

## ◼ Erotic Instructions:

Have your man sit on the bed with his legs extended in front of him. Crawl up to him on your knees and straddle him, lowering yourself onto his erect penis. Once you're comfortable, arch into a back bend—but be careful not to strain your lower back. Rest your head between his legs on the bed and reach your hands back to grab hold of his ankles or feet. That's when he leans forward and the fun begins.

## ◼ Why You'll Love It:

For those who are limber enough to last for even a few moments, the payoff is incredible. Throw your head back, close your eyes, and totally let go, because this position will connect you two like no other. Use his legs to brace yourself and add more oomph when you thrust. After this, your man will bend over backward for another all-out sexy panorama of your naked body in his hands.

**COSMO HINT** For a little extra support, place his hands so they grip you firmly underneath your lower back. To bring you two even closer together, ask him to slowly lean down and kiss your chest, carefully pulling your stomach up toward him in the process.

# Time Bomb

## ■ Erotic Instructions:

Have him sit down in a low chair with his legs relaxed. Facing him, straddle him with your feet on the floor, slowly lowering yourself onto his erection with your knees bent at a ninety-degree angle. Start by letting just the tip of his penis enter you, then lower yourself inch by inch until you're allowing him full entry by bearing all the way down on his thighs.

## ■ Why You'll Love It:

This is a highly affectionate pose with maximum upper-body contact, which naturally lends itself to languid kissing, hugging, and caressing. Best of all, since you're in the driver's seat you can stay in sync with him, so as a final reward you may be able to experience that explosive, but often elusive, moment: the simultaneous orgasm! This racy rendezvous is a surefire way for combustible carnal results.

**COSMO HINT**

To get the timing just right to O in unison, simply slow down your movements and let his fingers work their magic stimulating your clitoris if you sense he's on the verge. Once you're at the same pleasure point, get ready for a really big bang.

# Side Wind-her

## ■ Erotic Instructions:

Lie on your side and raise your top leg, keeping your bottom leg straight on the bed. Your man straddles your bottom thigh and hugs your raised leg as you rest your calf on his shoulder. Once he enters you, have him wind and whirl his hips as he thrusts for maximum pleasure.

## ■ Why You'll Love It:

All that gyrating ensures that your man's every thrust hits a new pleasure zone inside you, keeping you on the edge of ecstasy and 100% satisfied. Plus, he'll love the carnal control and being able to take in the lusty landscape of all your sexiest spots. Since he's enjoing being the power behind this position, let him do the work while you lie back, relax, and get your moan going.

**COSMO HINT** Since he's on his knees, have your partner alternate between a high kneeling position and a low crouch to add even more surprising sensations. The lower he goes, the deeper he gets—test different levels to discover what feels best.

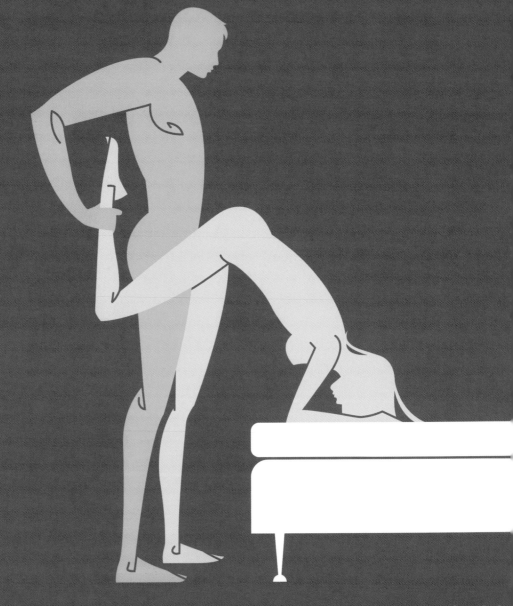

# Wanton Wheelbarrow

## ■ Erotic Instructions:

Start by standing and facing a bed or a chair. Bend over until your head and arms are resting on its surface. Have your man stand behind you and grab one of your ankles. Make sure to keep your knee slightly bent as you shift your weight to the leg that's still on the ground. Lifting your foot to rest near his hip, he should enter you from behind.

## ■ Why You'll Love It:

The Wanton Wheelbarrow is a rockin' alternative for those addicted to the angles and impact of any from-behind ride. Because your legs are pointed in opposite directions—one in the air and one on the ground—he's in perfect position to hit that oh-my-God G-spot. Plus, your man will be seriously turned on by the access to your posterior—have him give you a mini rear rubdown.

**COSMO HINT**

Get the Wanton Wheelbarrow on a roll by coordinating your thrusts. As he propels his hips forward, answer back with your booty by straightening your supporting leg. The two of you will meet in the middle for one hell of a ride that might just last all night!

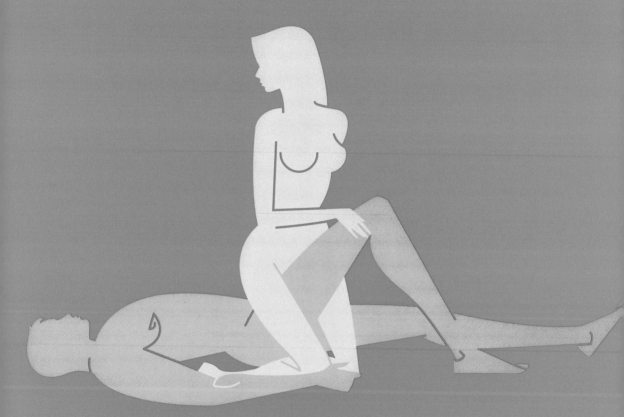

# Thigh Master

## ■ Erotic Instructions:

If you're bored with the standard woman-on-top pose, this position is a fun, frisky way to mix things up. Your guy lies on his back, one leg outstretched and the other bent, knee pointing upward. You straddle his body sideways with your back turned slightly to his face, hold on to his knee, and lower yourself onto his penis. In this pose, your stomach is almost touching his bent knee; use it for support and leverage as you rock back and forth, and up and down.

## ■ Why You'll Love It:

This torrid two-in-one move is all about your ecstasy. The steady rocking motion and thrusting create a pleasure buildup that primes you for the Big O. And you can thrill him by wrapping your hands around his legs and treat him to a titilating thigh massage. Gently knead those over-worked muscles then stroke his skin from knee to groin using firm feel-good pressure.

**COSMO HINT**

This is a primo pose for clitoral stimulation, so take full advantage by leaning far enough forward so your joy button rubs against his inner thigh. You control the motion in this pose, so mix up the speed and direction of your moves to get yourself off and keep your stud guessing.

# X Marks the Spot

## Erotic Instructions:

Lie back on your bed (or on any soft surface) with a pillow placed under your head. Bring your knees up to your breasts and cross your legs at your ankles. Your guy kneels right in front of you with his legs touching, leans in, and pulls your hips onto his angled lap. Keep your thighs glued together and gently press your feet against his chest for leverage as he slowly enters you. You can stroke his thighs as he moves back and forth with steady, ultrasnug thrusts.

## Why You'll Love It:

What makes this carnal connector a triple treat is the fire-starter friction created by crossing and clamping your legs together. That super rub-a-dub means more sensation for you both. Plus, this compact pose increases your ability to contract your PC muscles—which when tightened can heighten his pleasure by squeezing his penis, and yours by creating more awesome tension in your nether regions. This comprises all the ingredients for an especially intense buildup to a body-shuddering climax.

**COSMO HINT** You'll have an excellent view of your man in action, so enjoy the eye-candy, then whisper a word of praise for his tensed chest and built biceps—sexy compliments will fuel his fire.

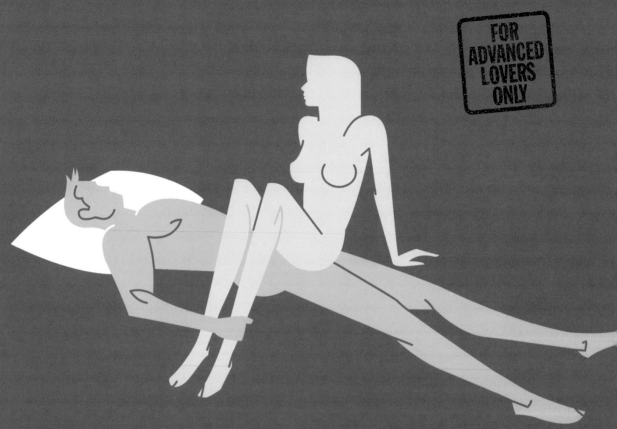

# Twirl-a-Girl

## ■ Erotic Instructions:

Have your partner lie on his back with his legs spread slightly and his head propped up with a pillow. Swing your legs over his body crosswise and keep them close together so your legs are positioned perpendicular to his. Sitting on top of his thighs or in his lap, lean back on your arms for maximum support. As he enters you, open your legs slightly and begin making slow, swiveling corkscrew motions.

## ■ Why You'll Love It:

If his head is propped up with a pillow, he can watch you as you move up, down, and around his penis—a surefire guy turn-on. Seeing you work your magic on his member will have him hot and heavy and dying to touch you. It's your choice: Let him get his mitts on you, telling him when and how you crave caressing; or ban his hands, teasing him into a frenzy.

**COSMO HINT**

Because you're on top, you're in control of the depth, speed, and intensity of the action. So if you sense he's about to lose it and you haven't yet arrived, simply slow down and set a new pace. In this position, there's plenty of potential for a dual-orgasm delight.

# Up, Up, and Away

## ■ Erotic Instructions:

Lie on your back with a pillow under your head, your legs in the air as straight and high as possible. While kneeling (his chest at your calves), your guy pushes your legs to one side slightly—not allowing them to flop all the way over—leans forward, and enters you. He can place his hands on the bed or floor on either side of your torso for support.

## ■ Why You'll Love It:

Keeping your legs up high and close together creates a super-tight fit, which means goose-bump-inducing friction for you and your man. And since he's entering you at a slight (about thirty-degree) angle, you both get a down-there sensation that's very distinct from what you're used to in the missionary or doggy position. You can stroke your own bliss button while your man pumps away, or just lie back, luxuriate in how oh-so-fabulous your body feels, and know that the view of you writhing in ecstasy is also making him howl.

**COSMO HINT** Experiment with alternating bending your knees a bit, and opening your legs slightly; with each move, you'll both experience a whole different grip and feel. Since the snug fit will loosen a little and the angle of entry will change, mixing things up this way will make your desire seriously take flight.

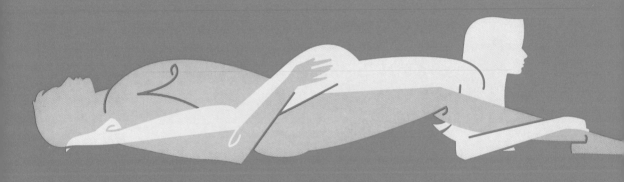

# The X-Rated

## ■ Erotic Instructions:

This position is all about control—so take it from the get-go and have your man lie faceup on the bed. Turn around and straddle him—so your back is toward him—and then lower yourself onto his erect penis. Extend your legs back toward his shoulders, relaxing your torso onto the bed between his feet. With both your legs and your man's forming an X-shape, start to slide up and down. Use his feet for added thrusting leverage.

## ■ Why You'll Love It:

Who said guys are the only ones who love X-Rated things? This position gives you total control, so experiment with different types of stimulation to see what pleases you both most. Your man will love relinquishing power and watching you take charge of your own orgasm. It doesn't hurt to add some X-Rated noises, letting him know just how good he feels.

**COSMO HINT**

Keep things moving in all directions. Use your vaginal muscles and move your buttocks up and down or back and forth to heighten the sensation even more. It's up to you to decide what to do. To him, nothing could be steamier than a sexy woman calling the shots.

# Mermaid

## ■ Erotic Instructions:

Lie faceup at the edge of a bed, desk, or countertop. Place a pillow under your butt to get some elevation. Extend your legs straight up, keeping them close together. You can put your hands under the pillow to raise your pelvis even higher, use them to hold on to the counter or desk for leverage, or keep them free. Your partner then enters you while standing up; if the bed or desk is low, he can kneel on the floor. He can grip your feet for leverage, which will give him the extra stability he needs to thrust more deeply.

## ■ Why You'll Love It:

Keeping your legs together means he feels fuller inside you, so you're creating lots of blissful friction and an incredibly tight fit. Give him a show and drive yourself wild by stimulating your clitoris while he's thrusting away.

**COSMO HINT** Occasionally separate your legs and bring them back together to get that first-tight-fit feeling again and again. The tight . . . tighter . . . tightest sensation will drive your guy wild, and the rush you'll get from calling the shots will create waves of pleasure.

# FIXES FOR YOUR WORST SEX FLUBS

Cosmo comes to the rescue with mattress-mess Rx for the most common crimes of passion.

| SEX FLUB | FAST FIX |
| --- | --- |
| "We always argue about who sleeps on the wet spot mess after sex." | Slip something super-soft yet absorbent like a terry blanket between your bodies and the bedding to keep the sheets dry. |
| "Once, during a sack session, my man's slapjacket slipped off and got stuck inside me." | Squat and pull it out. Next time, tell your man not to use too much lube inside of his condom. The extra moisture could cause it to slide off. |
| "He claims he loves the sight of my booty—but that rear-vealing walk from the bedroom to the bathroom is still mortifying." | Wrap yourself in a sexy cover-up that conceals your least-favorite ass-et, or throw on his shirt to hide your tush. |
| "After a hot night of knocking boots, I sometimes reach for my diaphragm, only to find out it's MIA." | Squat down and flex your PC muscle, then turn your finger deep inside your vagina, hook it onto the diaphragm's rim, and pull. |
| "Following a night of partying, my man wants to cuddle but his breath is rank." | Slip a morning mint from your mouth to his while you lock lips. |
| "The morning after a lusty night, my once perfect makeup creates an unappealing pasty mess across my face." | Use a cleansing towelette for quick clean-up. In the future, forgo everything except a little mascara. A post-O glow does a great makeup job. |

# The Sexiest Things to Do After Sex

He's sleepy, you're snuggly—
these tips will satisfy you both.

■ The post-sex scene: "Following intercourse, the male brain often goes into a rest state—he feels drained and tired—while the woman's brain is stimulated and intensely desires bonding," explains Michael Gurian, therapist.

We've identified afterplay pleasers that will bliss you *both* out.

### Pay Him a Compliment

Your flattering feedback will keep him from dozing—he's definitely gonna stay awake for this performance assessment—and kick-start light conversation, which you're probably in the mood for following a randy romp.

Plus, there's a long-term benefit to this booty wrap-up: It imprints your "Yes, please!" moments in his memory for next time.

### Give Him a Massage

This is a great way to maintain that physical connection for you and prolong his buzz. Obviously, foreplay hot spots—such as his privates—will be a tender no-go zone. For a more relaxing and sensual session, "Trace light circles on his torso. Starting at the chest, move around the navel, skim the pelvic bone, and continue back up," says Steve Capellini, massage therapist. "Or stroke your fingertips from his collarbone over his chest to his hip bones."

## CRASH OR DASH?

A guy is less likely to sleep over after a one-night stand because the hormone oxytocin (which makes him all lovey-dovey) fades fast following sexual release.

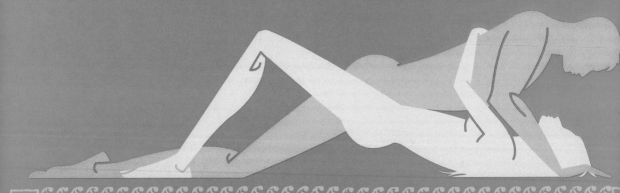

# Torrid Triangle

## ■ Erotic Instructions:

At first glance, you might think this is just the same routine missionary position with him on top and you on the bottom. But, of course, there's a secret Cosmo superlift twist! With you underneath him, ask him to get up on all fours. Then raise your pelvis up to meet his penis. Tell him he has to stay put as you start moving your fanny up and down to get frisky.

## ■ Why You'll Love It:

Don't be fooled by being on the bottom—you're definitely the one calling all the shots here. By lifting your pelvis, you're in charge of the speed and timing of every thrust—so move according to your wanton whims. What's more, as long as he obeys your stay-still orders, you also decide the depth of the penetration—the harder you push, the deeper he goes and the more you (both) moan.

**COSMO HINT**

Take a moment and enjoy your power trip! Here's your chance to tease him mercilessly by thrusting only halfway onto him. This will concentrate all sensations on the supersensitive tip of his tool. Then, when he least expects it, take the plunge and go all the way for a suprise rush of pleasure.

# Sneak-a-Peek

### Erotic Instructions:

Choose a sturdy, flat surface (like a kitchen counter or table) that hits him at hip level. Then do a striptease for him and hop onto the surface, placing your butt so it hangs just off the edge. While he stands in front of you, slowly lie back to give him a very special show. Prop yourself up on your elbows, spread your legs, and lift them so he can hold your calves or ankles.

### Why You'll Love It:

From this position, you'll get to see all the action and the delight on his face as he admires your beautiful package—face, breasts, tummy, and privates—from head to toe. Give him something to *really* drool over by occasionally throwing your head back and arching, so even more of you is on view.

**COSMO HINT**

Raise the visual stakes by reaching for his penis, withdrawing it from you, and running it up and down your inner labia (lingering on your clitoris) before you allow him to enter you again. Do it a couple of times and the start-stop build-up will have him boiling over with lust.

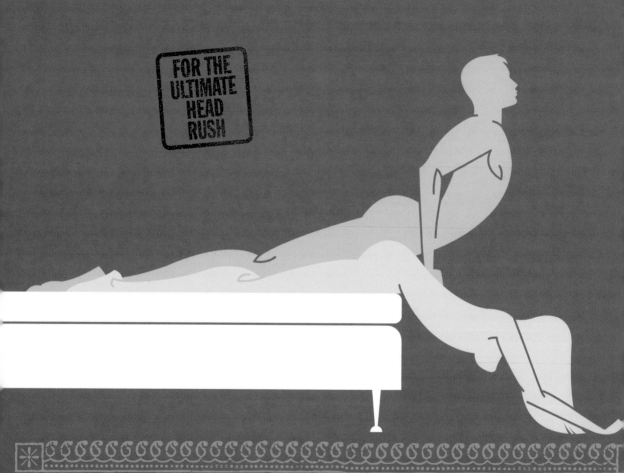

# Yes! Yes! Yes!

## ■ Erotic Instructions:

Lie facedown on the bed, then scoot your body forward so your head and torso hang over the side, your palms on the floor supporting your weight. Your man crawls over you and enters you from behind, his legs inside yours. He can hold on to your hips for leverage to allow him to keep his head and shoulders raised high instead of resting on your back. Your bodies will form a sideways Y, for Yes!

## ■ Why You'll Love It:

With your guy's legs confined between yours, you'll be treated to lots of quick, in-and-out moves—sending a tsunami of sensation to the nerve-rich first few inches of your pleasure zone. And because of the upside-down pose, the instant blood rush to your head will heighten each thrust, giving you a sort of out-of-body erotic experience. Because of the tricky configuration, this isn't a position you can linger in all night. But it adds a lot of adventure to a run-of-the-mill romp.

**COSMO HINT**

Wrap your ankles around his calves to "lock" him in place, then both of you grind in tight feel-good circles for a mind-blowing randy-region mesh. The close contact is perfect position for deep, daring sex. So close your eyes and just go with the flow—Yes! Yes! Yes!

# Love Triangle

## ■ Erotic Instructions:

Lie on your back on the floor or the bed with your left leg sticking straight up in the air. Take your right leg and stretch it out to your right side, so that it rests at a ninety-degree angle to your body. Reach across the floor with your right hand and clasp your right knee, forming a triangle on the bed with your right side, right leg, and right arm. Have your partner crouch at the bottom of your body and enter you.

## ■ Why You'll Love It:

The Love Triangle will totally redefine his idea of a three-way. This crouching position improves his pelvic control like nothing else, giving him the chance to thrust and touch you in ways you've never felt before. With your left hand, reach between his legs and stroke your nails through his pubic hair, gently tugging on a few strands while he works his magic.

**COSMO HINT**

Encourage him to take that added groin power and work it! Do a little show before you tell, gyrating your hips to get the motion down. Then, ask him to circle slightly as he thrusts—the friction from the conflicting movements will heat things up immeasurably.

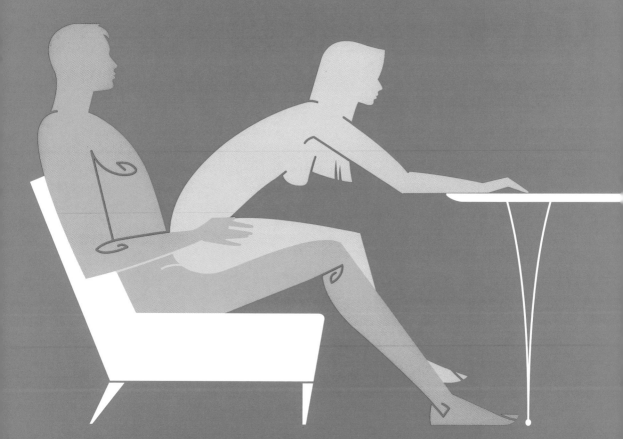

# Desk Detail

## ■ Erotic Instructions:

Sit your man down in a desk chair, with his legs spread out comfortably in front of him and his feet on the floor. Standing between his legs with your back to him, lower yourself down onto his lap. Once he's inside you, lean forward and stretch out your arms until they reach the desktop. Lift your feet up, suspending them in the air. He grabs your hips tightly and thrusts in small circles while you keep your legs together.

## ■ Why You'll Love It:

Who said desk duty was boring? Get ready to be brought to bliss because in this position, your guy is definitely the boss—literally. But unlike typical doggy-style sex, which can be hard on the knees, your guy can sit back, relax, and concentrate on taking you to incredible orgasmic heights. If he lifts your body up a bit as he thrusts, he can watch himself as he enters you—an experience guys all crave.

**COSMO HINT** To earn some extra erotic credit, ask your man to tilt you forward a bit more and shift the motion by using circular strokes. The twists and turns of this passion project will have you definitely wanting to stay late at the office.

# Baby Got Back

## ◼ Erotic Instructions:

Your best boy kneels, sitting back on his heels. With your back to him, you lower yourself onto his penis in a plié or squat, with your feet planted on either side of his legs. Placing your hands on your thighs for balance (he can place his hands on your rear for serious support), take him in only about a third of the way. Tease him for a few minutes, then gradually go deeper until you're nesting in his lap, the backs of your thighs and tush curving into him.

## ◼ Why You'll Love It:

This is one hell of a chick-in-charge pose, and there's nothing like having him beg for just an inch or two more. That whimpering you'll hear is his delight as he gets a full rear view of you and feels the pleasure of long, superorgasmic strokes once you start to pump up and down.

**COSMO HINT** For maximum erotic exposure, try this in front of a mirror so you can both watch as you gradually grind your way onto his lap. There's nothing hotter than witnessing a sexy session in progress, especially when the action is all yours.

FOR
LIMBER
LOVERS
ONLY

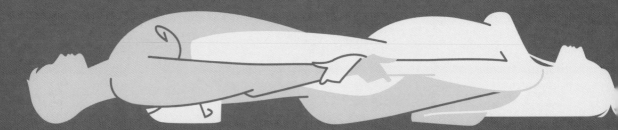

# Torrid Tug-of-War

## ■ Erotic Instructions:

Have him sit cross-legged on the floor or the bed before you straddle him. Lower yourself onto his penis and wrap your legs around his back. As you're sitting face-to-face, grab each other's elbows and lean back against the other person's weight—like a coy tug-of-war game. If you're limber enough, you might be able to tilt your head far enough back to rest it on the floor. Try to keep as still as possible, concentrating on you and your man's bodily connection.

## ■ Why You'll Love It:

This position is the perfect way to up the intimacy of any sexual encounter. Incorporate it for just a minute to meet mentally with one another. It's a calming connection and a great way to build momentum for the rest of the ride.

**COSMO HINT**

For this pose to work, you'll both need to keep your below-the-belt regions extra-meshed. If you feel yourselves slipping, use your arms to pull closer and maintain that all-important carnal connection. Do it right and this is one erotic game you'll both win.

# Niagara Falls

## ■ Erotic Instructions:

Facing the faucet, kneel in a tub that's already filled with warm water. Inch up so your body is very close to the water flow, then lean forward and hold the wall or sides of the tub for balance. Your guy climbs in behind you and, also kneeling, enters you from behind. As he thrusts, guide the water stream with your hand from the faucet or detachable showerhead between your legs.

## ■ Why You'll Love It:

This supersensual sex style is great for girls who don't always orgasm easily. You get a double-blissful whammy: Your man has prime G-spot access, while the water spray electrifies your external passion button. And with your bodies meshed tight in the tub, your guy can fondle your breasts and stroke you below the belt as he thrusts. All these ultra-arousing sensations—plus the sexy feel of warm water surrounding you on all sides—will take you into the deep end. Trust us, you'll never look at your tub the same way again!

**COSMO HINT**

Have him grab the soap and lather up his hands before slipping and sliding them around your body. His wet and wild touches will add an extra-sexy sensation and your skin will feel supersmooth. Just make sure you have a rubbery bath mat to keep the two of you steady.

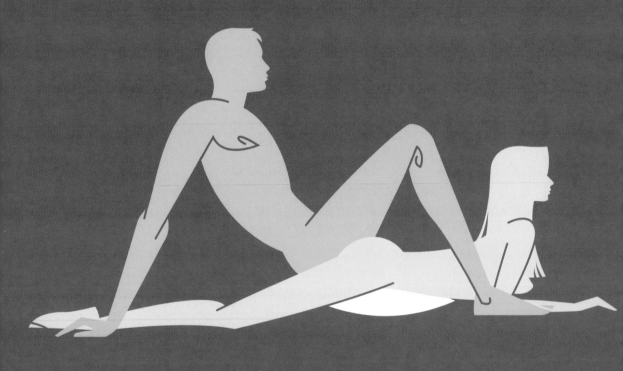

# Electric Slide

## ■ Erotic Instructions:

You lie down on the bed or the floor on your stomach, with your legs straight and slightly apart. Your guy sits right behind your buns (between your thighs) with his legs in front of him and his hands on either side of his body for support. He leans back at a forty-five-degree angle to your body so he can join his genitals with yours. As he rocks forward and back, bring your legs together for a tight fit. Rest on your elbows with your arms in front of you for leverage.

## ■ Why You'll Love It:

If your guy likes taking charge in bed, this position will let him be your passion pilot. He can glide back and forth as fast or sensually slow as he desires down the runway of your thighs. And since you're restricted from thrusting and grinding, you get to relax and completely relinquish control—allowing you to concentrate entirely on your pleasure. Plus, you get to enjoy the überhot element of surprise since you can't see which naughty nooky move he's planning to do next.

**COSMO HINT**
To add some extra sparks to this already electric pose, arch your back as much as possible. The change in position will cause your vaginal muscles to tighten, driving him wild!

# Standing Tiger/ Crouching Dragon

## Erotic Instructions:

Pose on all fours with your knees at the edge of the bed while your tiger stands behind you, his feet hip width apart. While he spreads his legs on either side of yours, keep your knees together to narrow your vaginal canal, causing it to feel much snugger around his penis as he thrusts. Be sure to let out a fiery dragon's roar to let him know how you feel!

## Why You'll Love It:

You get to focus on your own climax: You can easily reach your clitoris with one hand, and with his penis angled to hit the front wall of your tightened vagina, you're in perfect position for generous G-spot stimulation. And with his hands on your hips, he gets pleasure from controlling the angle and pace of thrusting—a take-charge role he won't be able to resist. It's a win–win sexual situation.

**COSMO HINT**
This is another perfect position that makes squeezing your PC muscles a major plus. The move will add imaginary inches to his member (a turn-on for both parties!). And all that tightening and releasing will slowly build up into one fantastic finale.

# The Erotic End

## ■ Erotic Instructions:

Sit your lover on the floor with his legs stretched out comfortably in front of him. Have him lean back slightly, using his arms to support his weight. With your back to him and your legs straddling his thighs, lower yourself onto him. Keep your knees bent and your feet planted on the floor. With your groins grinding together, squeeze your PC muscles while he makes small circular rotations with his pelvis.

## ■ Why You'll Love It:

With you on top, sometimes hitting your G-spot can be a little tricky. But turn your back on him (in a good way!) and the whole landscape changes. This position keeps you in control but affords him a much more direct shot at your can't-take-it-anymore zone. Meanwhile, he can kiss your neck, caress your inner thighs, and stroke other easy-to-access erogenous areas.

**COSMO HINT**

As if you on top isn't a turn-on enough, you can drive your man wild with your free hands. Tease his testicles with a few fingers or reach back to play with his nipples. Your guy is guaranteed to be beaming after this star-studded ride.